Bird Haunts in Southern England

by the same author

———

BIRD PHOTOGRAPHY
BIRD LIFE IN TWO DELTAS

BIRD HAUNTS
IN SOUTHERN ENGLAND

by

G. K. YEATES, B.A., F.R.P.S.

FABER AND FABER LIMITED
24 Russell Square
London

First published in Mcmxlvii
by Faber and Faber Limited
24 Russell Square London W.C.1
Second impression December Mcmxlvii
Printed in Great Britain by
Latimer Trend & Co Ltd Plymouth

To
K. and C. C.

*A very humble token
of my gratitude for all
their kindness to me
at Norwich*

Contents

Contents

Illustrations

9

Preface

The following pages are sketches of bird life as I have been fortunate enough to experience it in certain bird-haunts of Southern England south of a line from the Wash to the Severn, and particularly in the south-west where for some years I have lived. They were written largely while I was serving in the Army, in the leisure hours of winter evenings in barracks, when often nostalgia descended upon me and I longed once again to hunt for birds in an Exmoor coomb, to fight my way through a Sedgemoor osier-bed or to revel in the open spaces of a Salisbury Plain that did not reek of military manœuvres and gas courses.

These places I have loved, and although I have been frequently tempted away from them by the lure of Mediterranean delta or northern island and moor, it is amongst their birds that I have spent most of my time. In pursuit of rarities or of birds of other climes I have never under-estimated my debt to the woodlands, fields and downs, the marshes, heaths and hedgerows of Southern England. I can only hope that this book will reflect a little of the joy and pleasure I have had in searching for their birds, both common and rare.

I am a bird photographer, and my hobby I regard as a field sport. This attitude, which recognizes the fascination and the excitement of the chase and of the hunt, it is fashionable to-day amongst serious ornithologists to reject. We are told that unless our observations are 'useful', we waste our time. For myself I confess that while I hope that in the pursuit of my quarry I still keep my eyes open to observe, yet I am in no way worried if at the end of the hunt I have seen little that has not been seen or recorded before. So long as birds are, as to the great majority indeed they are, a hobby and a means of relaxation, I shall not blush at such an

Preface

attitude, though its reactionary nature may be the despair of my more serious friends.

This book is therefore merely a record of my personal experiences of the birds with which I have dealt. Much of my work has been complicated by photographic problems and such difficulties as the construction and introduction of hides. These matters, however, being of interest only to those who are bitten with the bird-photographic bug, I have kept as far as possible in the background. If they have entered in larger part into the last chapter, it is because in the case of the black redstarts of Lowestoft they are very much part of the story.

My debts of gratitude are numerous. A bird photographer can only rarely work alone. Apart from practical assistance in his actual work he is frequently indebted to friends who write to tell him of the discovery of a bird or even of its nest; to others for information about localities; or to landowners for permission to enter their property. Indeed it is almost impossible to photograph any bird without incurring a debt of gratitude. All those who have assisted me in obtaining the photographs which illustrate this book I would thank most deeply. I can only hope that they will not think their good offices have been entirely in vain. On one score at least they can rest assured—the great personal pleasure the taking of these photographs has given me. In that they have played a greater part than perhaps they may realize, and for it I would thank them all very genuinely.

G. K. YEATES.

Sherborne, 1946.

14

CHAPTER 1

Norfolk Reed-Beds

O f all British bird sanctuaries the Norfolk Broads are the most famous. The last extensive remnant of the old fen country which once covered much of East Anglia, they have to this day preserved within their reed-beds, marshes and waterways a home for many species which, if not all exclusively confined to them, are yet there to be found at their numerical peak. Not all bird sanctuaries can claim such variety. Dungeness is associated with the Kentish plover; Hermaness with the great skua; Rothiemurchus with the crested tit; but Hickling and Horsey do not rely for their reputation on any one single species. They are the only remaining breeding haunt of the two or three pairs of marsh harriers which nest in Britain; of the bittern and of the bearded tit they are the stronghold. Add to these celebrities the presence in most seasons of Montagu's harrier and short-eared owl, of water rails in abundance and of nearly all the marsh and aquatic birds in great numbers, and it is not difficult to realize why the Norfolk Broads have become so famous a Mecca for British ornithologists.

Yet it can only be with the greatest diffidence that he who is able to pay but fleeting visits to the Broads writes of their bird-life. At best he can give only mere impressions and make but a humble contribution to their ornithology, for the birds of Broadland live out their lives screened by the reed and sedge forests in which they nest. When a man of such unrivalled opportunities and of so keen an eye as the late Jim Vincent could say of the bittern that although he had first found its nest over thirty years ago, and had been trying to fathom its ways ever since, it was still almost as great a mystery to him in 1941 as it was in 1911, the

15

picture which a mere fortnight will give the casual visitor will obviously be fleeting and very incomplete. A month with such birds as the Shetland skuas or the Highland dotterel and ptarmigan can lead to a working knowledge of their habits, for except for their remoteness these birds conduct their lives in the open. But the bittern and the bearded tit live hidden by the great reed-beds and are often no more than unseen voices in the undergrowth.

The bittern is for me *the* bird of Broadland. Perhaps the marsh harrier or the bearded tit should hold the place of honour, for they are exclusive to it, while the bittern has extended its range to other nesting haunts. But it was from Hickling that this expansion began: it is at Hickling that to-day it is most easily seen and found: it is the bittern's boom that above all other noises is the orchestral background of the Broads. The cacophonous music of reed and sedge warblers, the grunting of water rails, the yodelling of redshank, the violin-plucking of the bearded tit, all these are essential features of the general chorus. But as you stand by the Broads' edge on a spring evening, it is the far-carrying booming of the bitterns that you will hear and that you will retain as the most vivid impression.

While I was sitting in my hide over a bittern, I kept careful notes of the occurrence of this most strange sound. The male bird, which I presumed to belong to my nest, had his station in the same reed-bed and did his booming at distances of about twenty to two hundred yards from the nest itself, but the sound is so ventriloquial in its effect that its distance away can at best only be estimated. When the booming bird is close, however, much else can be heard besides the actual boom. It begins with two or three quiet clicking noises, as though the boomer had a slight obstruction and was clearing its respiratory passages. There follow two or three deep inspirations. Then comes one boom; another inspiration; a second boom; another inspiration; and a third boom. A three-boom delivery takes about three and a half to four seconds to complete.

At the height of the breeding season, when only I know it, the bittern's boom is usually three-fold, but four-fold is not uncommon. Two I have heard, but never five, though as many as nine have been recorded. Standing on the edge of Hickling one April evening, for instance, I counted in twelve booms in twenty minutes from various bitterns, four four-fold, eight three-fold; and although I took no figures afterwards, the three-fold is clearly the commonest type. The four-fold

PLATE I. *Bittern at nest*

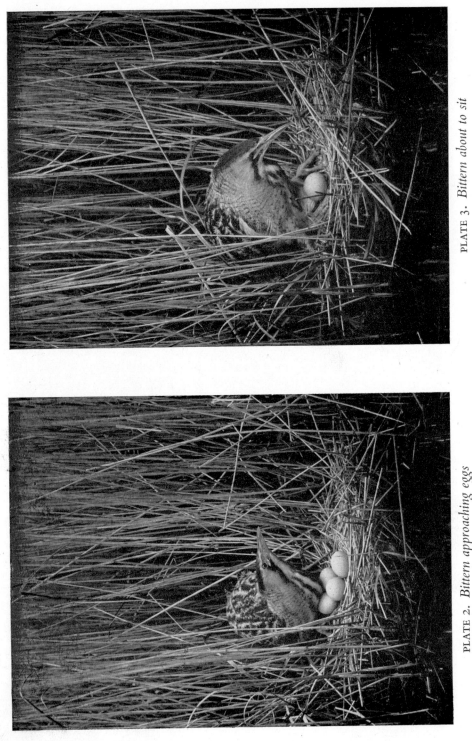

PLATE 3. *Bittern about to sit*

PLATE 2. *Bittern approaching eggs*

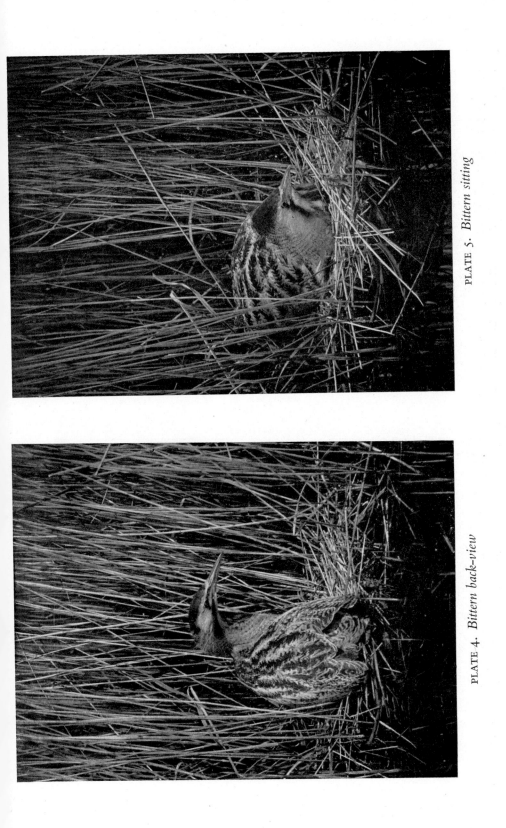

PLATE 5. *Bittern sitting*

PLATE 4. *Bittern back-view*

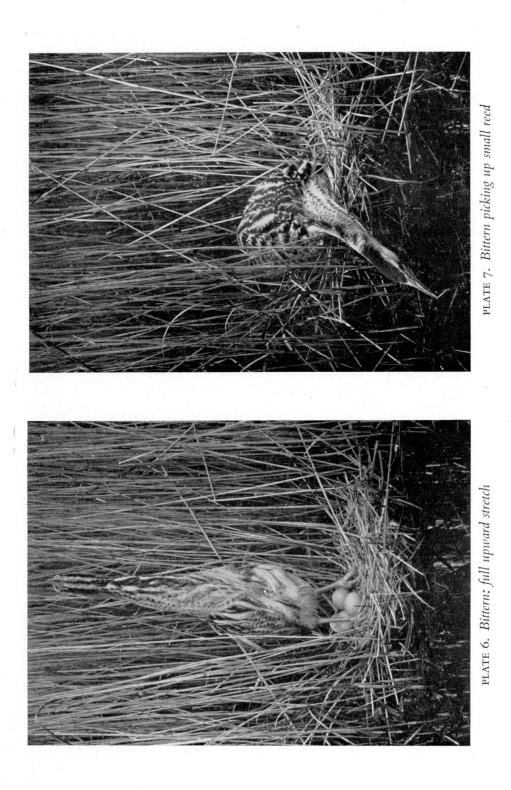

PLATE 7. *Bittern picking up small reed*

PLATE 6. *Bittern: full upward stretch*

PLATE 9. *Female Bearded Tit*

PLATE 8. *Male Bearded Tit*

PLATE 10. *Shoveler on nest*

PLATE 11. *Montagu's Harrier alighting at nest*

PLATE 12. *Montagu's Harrier and chicks*

booms seem to come from certain birds. In records of sixty-two booms from my own cock bird only two were three-fold; all the rest were four. Yet other males at various stations on the Broad which I could hear from my hide were three-boomers, and I only very rarely heard an occasional four, except from my bird. But—and it is here that the incompleteness of a brief visit is revealed—when the bittern starts booming, Jim Vincent informed me that it begins with very poor efforts, that they mount to a maximum and then decline. For all I know my bird may have reached its prime before its rivals. A mere fortnight was too short to tell.

The volume of booming is perhaps greatest in the evening, and my records seem to indicate that the bird is in best voice when it is cool. Here is a summary of one day's booming (26th April). The hours are B.S.T.

10.45—11.45	7 booms	warm
11.45—12.45	4 booms	very warm and still
12.45— 1.45	5 booms	very warm
1.45— 2.45	8 booms	warm: getting cooler
2.45— 3.45	4 booms	cooler
3.45— 4.55	15 booms	cool

A sudden period of cool in the middle of a hot day will also occasion an outburst. On one such day I have a record of ten booms per hour in a cool spell at mid-day.

It seems perhaps possible to correlate booming with the presence or absence of the hen at the nest. I kept notes of this when recording the booms, and on the day above detailed, of the 43 booms recorded 39 were made when the female was sitting, or in the vicinity of the nest, 4 when she was off the eggs—but then she was sitting all day except for the period 2.45—3.45 p.m. It is however suggestive that in a period when the cock (1.45—4.55 p.m.) was with the cooling of the temperature clearly waxing into good voice, he relapsed for the one hour when his wife was off the nest, probably feeding and perhaps in his company. The sitting female however takes not the least notice of her husband's musical efforts.

Booming is not the bittern's only means of vocal expression. The highlight of my hours at close quarters with the bittern was provided on the day when I was fortunate enough to have a visit to the nest from a cock bird. I have deliberately said *a* cock bird, because the male's presence at the nest is most unusual, and indeed Jim Vincent knew of no other record in his experience. He suggested therefore that this bird was perhaps not the legal male. I am however doubtful, for it is significant that while he was visiting the female, I have no record of a boom from 'my' cock bird in the reed-bed behind.

The female had been unusually long in returning to her eggs. At last without any warning—the silence of a bittern's movements in a reed-bed are not the least of its great mysteries—the reeds parted behind the nest, and she came on. She was clearly agitated. Normally a more stolid, docile old lady it would have been difficult to imagine. On this occasion something was obviously disturbing her, and as she sat, she kept up a subdued chorus of gruff notes, as though she were intensely annoyed or upset.

Suddenly to my amazement I heard confident strides through the reeds and water behind my hide. These were none of the splashings and disturbances of the waterhens which shared the reed-bed and to the noise of whose activities I was by now accustomed. Something much larger was approaching. It was another bittern. The bird on the nest grew very agitated, and began a loud and incessant *tchutta-tchutta-tchutta*, uttered in threes with very little pause between each phrase. As the male reached the side of the hide, he flew the rest of the way and landed just beside the nest with a tremendous splash. The hen advanced to meet him, chittering loudly. Her attitude *looked* aggressive, but for all I know it may have been a female bittern's idea of a cordial reception.

There followed a period of great wing-beating and the excited chittering reached fever heat. In the general mêlée of wings and battered reeds it was difficult to follow events. The two birds finished in the main reed growth just to one side of the nest. The male bird, his wings outstretched in the reeds, his mane fluffed out, his feet supported on the reeds, was treading the female and at the same time feeding her by regurgitation. That much at least I could see. He was with her in all for three and a half minutes. Then he departed through the reeds with the same devil-may-care noise with which he had arrived.

The female was most upset by this unusual visit. For twelve minutes without a break she chittered behind the nest in her annoyance or pleasure. Indeed she did not return to her eggs for another twenty minutes. Even then for an hour after the incident there were occasional outbursts, as though the memory of the assault suddenly returned to her. It ended with a yawn—of resignation?

18

The male's visit was the only piece of dynamic action I saw. Few birds can be more placid or stolid than an incubating bittern. I have remarked already on the silence of her approach. A reed-bed is the most difficult place in the world in which to move quietly. A human being who *tries* to be quiet cannot do so. A bittern is a large bird, yet only the most intensive listening will give a clue of her coming—usually the slight splashes of water drops. Frequently the first warning I got was a long neck with thick orange bill coming through the screen of reeds behind the nest. It would be followed by a green foot which did not seem to mind if it were placed actually on the eggs; and at last the heavy, fat body.

A bittern can change its shape more completely than any bird I know. The normal incubating bird is a heavy, thick-set fowl, neck tucked into body. Every now and then, to pick up a floating reed or to arrange the nest, the bull-like neck is stretched out until it becomes a long, thin, scraggy thing of astonishing length. But this is as nothing to the at-tenuation which occurs when a human being approaches. At such times she may slip off quietly and retire through the reeds, but at others she will raise herself on tiptoe, make slim even her fat body and extend her neck bolt upright to an extent that only seeing will believe. Then is seen to advantage the wonderful adaptive coloration of the streaks on her throat and neck, which merge perfectly with the surrounding reeds. Then too is seen the comical sight of her binocular vision, as, bill point-ing skywards, she turns her eyes to see straight before her, round and under her bill. Truly a remarkable bird.

Time as always was my enemy, and I could not wait till the olive eggs hatched and the little brown golliwogs emerged. On that account I did not see the bittern's toilet—its powder-puffing and its use of the oil gland with which to restore to good order its neck and head feathers, made slimy by the death struggles of the eels it has killed. Lord William Percy has described and filmed this interesting event, but I had to leave before it was likely to occur at my nest. There were times when the sitting bird would be away from her eggs for long periods. I have no doubt that she was then feeding, doubtless also doing her toilet, but in the depths of the reed-bed, not at the nest, and therefore unseen by me.

That delightful little bird of the reed-beds, the bearded tit, is for me only a casual acquaintance. Yet it is a privilege to know it even *en passant,* for it is a rare bird which, even if it were abundant, would not

19

lose one iota of its fascination, so distinctive and beautiful is the male. Its status however is always uncertain, for it is at the mercy of the elements. Like the Dartford warbler it is a specialized insectivorous bird which does not attempt to escape the English winter by extensive migration. Like the Dartford also it has other enemies to its well-being. There are no heath fires on the Broads as there are on Surrey commons, nor are there tanks or military manœuvres; but there are floods and at times big incursions of salt water. Reed and sedge beds are cut and cleaned. Both of these alike can bring disaster to the bearded tit, for both can kill its food supply, especially salt water which does not discriminate. For the bearded tit seems to be a bird of a specialized habitat within a specialized haunt. To regard it as merely a bird of the Broads and of the reed-beds is to see but half the picture. Within those reeds and sedge beds it is still localized, preferring those with a mat of vegetation over shallow water which has not been cleared for three or four years. It seems that it is only after such a space of time that the insect which forms its staple diet, *Laverna phragmitella*, whose larvae burrow into the reed mace, really thrives in quantities to the bearded tit's liking.

It was in the appreciation of such subtleties as these that the true greatness of Jim Vincent, the famous Hickling keeper, was revealed. Vincent knew the bearded tit's requirements because he could—or so it seemed—think like a bearded tit. When he 'cut' Hickling, he cut in such a way as to leave at all times a number of beds which were in exactly the right state of growth and decay to suit the bearded tit.

To see how true was his knowledge of this little bird's ways it was only necessary to have the privilege of hunting in his company for a nest. In miles and miles of reed and sedge and waterways he would quant his punt to certain particular beds. We would pass many which to my inexperienced eyes looked identical with the one at which we finally stopped. Yet his instinct was sure, and in a good bearded year it was odd if there were not birds where he said they would be.

Yet if his prescience of the actual habitat was remarkable, it was as nothing to his uncanny ability actually to locate the nest. Vincent seemed to smell them. Doubtless he had his failures, but I never saw them. There is no royal road to success in the nest-finding of any bird. Nine-tenths of it is experience, and I have never seen that fact proved more clearly than by Jim Vincent and the bearded tit. It was an education and a privilege even once to be out with him on a bearded hunt.

PLATE 13. *Montagu's Harrier with full-fed young*

PLATE 14. *Montagu's Harrier at nest*

PLATE 15. *Bearded Tit country—Hickling Broad*

PLATE 16. *Crossbill country—Breckland*

With his death we have lost a very great field-naturalist, and the bearded tits of Hickling their most understanding friend. Fortunately he has passed on his discoveries; his experience he could not hand over, for time alone can give that, most precious of all knowledge.

If the bittern and the bearded tit are two certain objects of a bird-watcher's visit to the Broads, with them also must be coupled the harriers. Of the marsh harrier the Hickling-Horsey area is the only remaining nesting ground in Great Britain, and here there are usually two or three pairs, in some years even as many as five. Yet because of its great rarity and above all its excessively nervous temperament, so intolerant and so suspicious of interference, I have remained content with merely distant views of this great terror of the Broads, and I have inspected only two nests there after the eggs have been safely hatched. What little I know of the marsh harrier has been gleaned abroad in South France and Spain where the bird is as abundant as here it is rare.

Early in the breeding season I have watched at Hickling marsh harriers courting. The male bird, a really beautiful bird with very light head and shoulder patches (marsh harriers show very considerable variation in plumage) would mount high in the sky, so high indeed that he became a mere speck against the clouds. Here he would circle, the while uttering a thin and incessant cry which at the time I noted in my field notes as 'reminiscent of a little tern'. From the reed-beds beneath this would bring his lady up to meet him. Grand aerial displays followed—mutual circling, mutual diving. At times one bird would mount above the other, then both descend in spirals. On occasion the hen would turn up to meet his dive; there would be a mock 'pass', but I never saw real food given. On a sunny calm April day it is a sight upon which to feast the eyes— the rarest of British breeding birds at its best. Abroad I have seen it many times. Perhaps my insularity may be forgiven if I remember it most clearly at Hickling.

The same too holds good of the 'pass' which in the delta of the Rhône was a common sight. Yet I like to think of it in terms of the great male marsh harrier I saw one June day flying low over the Horsey reed-beds. In his talons he carried prey, and he was flying with a purpose. He seemed to cover miles of Broadland before he began to lift. It was any moment now, and doubtless, had he been nearer, I could have heard his food call to the brooding female. Suddenly a second heavy bird was in the air, mounting towards him . . . they closed for a moment . . . the food changed talons, and the hen returned to the reed bed from which she had come. There was a nest there, but it was not for me to disturb it.

Or again I like to think of another hot June afternoon when I found myself unexpectedly close to a female marsh harrier whose five chicks I had been privileged to inspect. She had circled over in anxiety, and I was left hidden in a line of trees to watch. Once the coast was clear, she came down to quarter her breeding marsh. Was it to look down into her nest for reassurance? At any rate her fears were apparently dispelled, for she alit on the dead branch of a tree near by and let my glasses sate themselves in admiring her grandeur.

Montagu's harrier is neither so temperamental a bird nor so confined in its breeding distribution. Indeed it does not nest every year in Broadland, and it is possible that parts of Devon and Cornwall hold more breeding pairs, while it breeds locally even as far north as Yorkshire. It is a most graceful bird, as buoyant as the marsh harrier is cumbersome, and a male Montagu, resplendent in his heron blue-grey, black-tipped wings, quartering the Broadlands marshes must always be one of the great sights of a bird-watcher's experience. A bird of the heath and moor as well as of the marsh, it is nevertheless at its best over the reeds and sedges on a bright summer day.

With the Montagu as a bird I had been long acquainted before I had the opportunity to see it at close quarters at the nest. For that I am greatly indebted to Major Anthony Buxton of Horsey, who with the late Lord Desborough and Jim Vincent at Hickling has done so much to protect both species of harrier and all the Broadland birds. Side by side with their great efforts stands in marked contrast the selfishness and narrow-mindedness of neighbouring estates which have not hesitated to shoot the young birds which have wandered from their native sanctuary, victims of misguided game-preservation. For all birds of prey, not least the harriers, require wide feeding grounds, and cannot be confined within a circumscribed area. Unfortunately birds cannot read danger notices, nor do they observe the boundaries of property or the laws of trespass. That they are killers of a high order no one who knows their ways would attempt to deny, but while they remain uncommon birds, is it too much to hope that the game-preserver will see the bigger picture and not merely his private shooting bag?

Of the effect of their depredations I have not the experience to speak. Vincent, who of all field-naturalists in this country should have the authority to speak, was himself convinced that the Hickling area could not support many pairs and that its small-bird life had been reduced by the coming of the harriers, a sacrifice to their encouragement and protection. At the same time I have seen harriers abroad in numbers unbelievable in this country, yet living and thriving side by side with a very varied and numerous bird population. In the Camargue, the delta of the Rhône, marsh harriers—Montagu is inexplicably a rare bird—*abound*. I once counted a score from one stand-point, and every fresh marsh I passed or inspected was well populated. Yet there was no shortage of small bird-life. Reed and sedge warblers in the reed-beds, coots, waterhens, grebes and many ducks in the fresh marshes, waders on the surrounding dried muds, flourished in great numbers despite the presence of so many harriers.

Even more striking was the case in Southern Spain where every marsh of any size, lagoon or river estuary seemed to form the haunt of numerous harriers of both species. Yet there were other birds, sharing these same haunts for nesting, and flourishing. One locality, the *marismas* of the Guadalquiver and the Coto Doñana, is indeed one of the most famous shooting paradises in Western Europe—despite the harriers. If these territories are of greater extent than Broadland, they also have to support a much greater population of the marauders, and they appear to do so without any disastrous effect upon the rest of their avifauna.

My glimpse of Montagu's harrier at the nest was brief—a mere forty-eight hours' leave, a gift from the military gods for VE day. The nest was typical—a platform in a tangled sedge-bed about hip-high—and it contained four chicks, of very different ages and sizes. Beside the prosperous, well-fed young gentleman who was clearly the eldest of the family, the youngest was a weakling, insignificant of size and mere scrag and bone, not even his white down fully developed. The treatment he received from his flourishing brethren would have been an education to those who cannot think of Nature except in terms of maudlin sentimentality. He was callously picked up by the scruff of his neck and pitched about the nest. When food arrived, he was trampled on. Even his mother paid him scant attention. I heard later that he died. I should have been surprised only if I had heard the contrary.

The practice is common to many birds of prey of hatching their eggs at intervals, as much as a week in the short-eared owl, but its biological significance is obscure. Is it an insurance against sudden failure of food supply at the vital stage, a precaution to make sure that at least one or two chicks per brood reach full-fed maturity if food becomes scarce when most needed? For if food is plentiful, it is by no means always the case that even these weaklings die. A marsh harrier's nest which I saw at this time held five chicks, the eldest of which was enormous when its youngest brother was hatched. Yet all five flew.

In all the harriers the share of the sexes in domestic duties is clearly defined. The nest is the female's province, although the male will visit it occasionally. His part is that of the bread-winner, both during incubation for the sitting female and after hatching for the chicks as well. In the later stages of the development of the young the female will sally forth and make her own kills, but such forays seem to be exceptional, and the provision of food can be regarded as the male's exclusive task.

His coming is the highlight of life at the nest. As he swings over, all the chicks peer eagerly upward, following his movements with ever-growing squeaks of anticipation. To the hen brooding or on guard near by he calls with a soft jackdaw-like *tchook-tchook*. At this signal she rises to meet him to take the food by a 'pass', returning to apportion it amongst the young.

On one occasion he flapped over the hide and called. The female standing on the edge of the nest screamed at him but would not leave. He returned, but still she would not leave, still screamed at him. A third time, and he hovered above the hide. The hen sprang into the air. Almost immediately a bird returned to the nest. I peeped through the hide to see the cock in all his glory on the edge. He was away almost before I had realized his presence, certainly long before I had time to release my camera shutter.

Ten minutes later I heard his food call again, and the female, who had returned in the meantime, left immediately without defiant screaming at him. This time I was determined not to be caught half-asleep. A bird thumped on to the nest. I peeped at it: it was the female—it would be! I imagined the cock had retired for further hunting. I exposed a plate. To my horror I had no sooner done so than the blue male descended and stood facing his lady on the far side of the nest. He gave one look at his chicks and in a trice was away! My language knew no bounds.

The following day he gave me a third glimpse in the evening. The female had left the nest, and when he came over with food, his call-notes failed to produce her. After two circuits he thumped on to the nest, dropped his food and was away. This time I did expose a plate, but the speed of both his coming and of his going was too great. I must however count myself extremely fortunate within two days to have had three visits to the nest from a male Montagu's harrier. I must also account myself a very bad bird photographer to have got nothing out of those opportunities.

To think of the Broads only in terms of bitterns and bearded tits, marsh and Montagu's harriers is to form a most incomplete picture, biased by the attraction of rarity. While the bittern's boom is *the* noise of the Broads and while the lazy flapping flight of the harriers over the reed beds is a characteristic feature, there is a great wealth also of more common birds. In the reeds, sedge and reed warblers keep up a constant chatter, and male reed buntings wheeze out their sleepy ditties. The quiet but far-carrying reeling of the grasshopper warbler is often heard, though the singer is rarely seen. Coots, waterhen and mallard are in the secluded pools, and on the open water great crested grebes are abundant. Strangely the watery 'neigh' of the dabchick is not one of the characteristic sounds of Broadland, at least at Hickling—an inexplicable exception. In the smaller marshes of low sedge and rough aquatic vegetation water rails 'grunt and groan' at human intrusion.

The water rail's vocabulary is surely one of the most astonishing of all birds'. I once spent a few hours close to a nest which was in the middle of hatching. When I arrived five of the original nine eggs were hatched, and while four of the delightful black young had already joined their parents—none of the eggs had been even chipped the evening before—one little black golliwog was still in the nest with the remaining four eggs. I expected great things, for water rails at the hatch are credited with tremendous activity—carrying their chicks and the like. But the day was scorching, and the rails waited behind the vegetation at the back of the nest and, as the eggs hatched in the heat of the sun, called their chicks into cover. I hardly saw the birds at all, but I was serenaded by an astonishing chorus of grunts, belches, groans, wheezes and the like. If any bird suffers from perpetual flatulence, it is the water rail. It suffers from continuous indigestion of the most acute order.

The tale of Broadland bird life is but half told if the birds of the marshes as opposed to the reed-beds are ignored. Lapwing, redshank and snipe are no peculiarities of the Broads; they are widely distributed, often in haunts very different, moorland bogs or chalk uplands. Here at

Hickling however their spring music is second only to the bittern's boom. Lapwing cart-wheeling over the rough fields, redshank yodelling in their beautiful courtship flight, snipe drumming, are on an April day the very spirit of a Broadland spring, and without them the marshes would be inestimably the poorer.

In the same fields as they favour nest also mallard and shoveler. While hunting for nests of redshank one day, I flushed a duck shoveler from a clutch of thirteen eggs in a tuft of rough grass. What a transformation there is when the dull browns of the duck, so perfectly adapted to concealment, on a sudden take wing and in their place a dozen olive eggs glare up at the sky! No wonder when the bird leaves at her leisure to feed she covers them carefully with down. I put a hide on this bird and in due course waited for the duck's return. She was conducted to the vicinity of the nest by the drake. On the first occasion he pitched with her about twenty yards away, waited till she was on and then departed: on others he accompanied her on the wing to the area of the nest, but when she pitched, he flew on, calling with a subdued, metallic quacking, *tchük-tchük*.

I will always remember the stealth of that old duck's approach. I would see nothing after she had pitched, until through the screen of grass round the nest a big spatulate bill protruded, then a soft, kind eye, followed by a brown body. I was never conscious of any movement in her progress. She seemed to slide imperceptibly on to the eggs and sit. I had to take my pictures quickly, for within a quarter of an hour she had screened herself out of direct view with the surrounding grasses that had been parted to expose her.

Broadland is not only a great breeding ground: it is also a great winter haunt and stopping place for migrants. The number of rare birds which Jim Vincent has recorded from Hickling is a testimony not only to his own quick eye and ability as a field-naturalist but also to its attraction for passing visitors. A day there at any time of the year is capable of producing great surprises. Only a month ago, as I write, I quanted to a piece of flood water from which rose six black birds, broad of wing and curved of beak, six large dark 'curlews', silhouetted against the sky—glossy ibises. Hungarians? Perhaps . . . who knows?

CHAPTER 2

Crossbills in Breckland

The crossbill, that beautiful bird of the northern pine forests, is a species much subject to fluctuations. Like the waxwing of the same forests or Pallas' sand-grouse from the east it appears to have seasons of sudden increase when it overflows in its native haunts and spreads in numbers into countries in which it is normally a rare bird. In the case of the crossbill these invasions are more regular than in either of the other two species mentioned, for it is rare for a decade to pass without at least one of its periodic visitations.

This habit is of no recent origin. It was sufficiently marked even in the thirteenth century to arouse the attention of Matthew Paris and to cause him to make mention of this bird in his otherwise historical chronicle. Yet the real historical background of birds goes back little more than a century, and it is difficult to obtain sound evidence of ornithological matters the other side of 1800. Although there are accepted records of the breeding of crossbills before 1839, that year would seem to be the first of which we can say that the crossbill came to nest with us in numbers.

From then until 1910 the bird 'irrupted' at intervals of three to ten years, but there were many seasons during those seventy years when the species does not seem to have bred at all. Following an invasion in 1909, a definite 'colony' varying from year to year in numbers, but never completely untenanted, was formed in the Breck country of Norfolk and Suffolk, for here since 1910 it has bred regularly, although in certain years, as for instance 1933-5, it has been very scarce. This district has apparently always suited the bird, for such well-attested records of the

27

breeding of crossbills that we have prior to the historical year of 1839 refer chiefly to these two same counties.

The crossbill under discussion is of course the common crossbill, *Loxia curvirostra curvirostra*. Side by side with this, the typical form of the species, there has existed from time immemorial in Britain a sub-species known to-day as the Scottish crossbill, *Loxia curvirostra scotica*. This bird, like the crested tit, is a relic of the old coniferous forests of Britain. With the reduction of the ancient forests it also retreated, until to-day it is found only in the far north. It has not however found it so difficult as the crested tit to adapt itself to changed circumstances, for while the latter is exclusively confined to the Spey valley, the forests of Rothiemurchus and Abernethy and in a lesser degree to the neighbouring Findhorn valley, the Scottish crossbill breeds from south-east Sutherland and Western Ross down to lower Perthshire. The ancient forest of Rothiemurchus is however its undoubted headquarters.

The position of the Scottish crossbill must nevertheless be regarded as unsatisfactory. That it should not always be separable in the field is a feature common to most sub-species. It is characterized by a heavier bill, sometimes very noticeably so. But when the greatest authority on bird skins, the late H. F. Witherby, can say in the latest and most authoritative book (*The Handbook of British Birds*) 'if it should be proved that the typical form also breeds regularly in the same area of the Highlands, this bird (Scottish crossbill) should be considered as a form of the parrot-crossbill', then indeed the layman is forced to wonder. For the parrot-crossbill, a bird with a much heavier bill, is a separate species, not a mere sub-species. Have we then here got a bird of which the authorities cannot even say to which *species* it belongs? We are bidden to regard it as a sub-species of the common crossbill, yet warned to hold ourselves in readiness to jettison that view and to accept it as the sub-species of a different and separate species! To one such as myself who is no taxonomist that appears to be a most unsatisfactory situation. Unfortunately proof would require the use of the gun. Better live crossbills and the point unsettled than a series of dead skins and a clear-cut decision.

The Scottish crossbill, however, whatever its correct place, is clearly a bird of long standing, and when we talk of crossbill irruptions and invasions in England, it must be remembered that all the time a comparatively static and geographically-isolated race of the bird has been existing side by side in the fir forests of the north, from which unlike its

PLATE 17. *Crossbill sitting*

PLATE 18. *Hobby with full-grown chicks*

Continental counter-part it rarely irrupts, although it has been identified in the Lowlands in winter.

With a species subject to such fluctuations it will be apparent that the
best opportunities for observing the bird nesting occur in the spring
following an invasion. Such occurred in 1936. From 1933 to 1935 the
crossbill nested only very sparingly in its 'headquarters colony' in Norfolk and Suffolk, but the autumn and winter of 1935 produced many and
widespread records of crossbill flocks in England. It was clear that an
irruption was in progress, and, having a friend who was a Forest Officer
on the borders of Norfolk and Suffolk, I decided in the spring of 1936
that an attempt should be made to see something of this interesting bird
at the nest.

Crossbills are early breeders. Records of January and February nests,
although they are common enough, have however hidden the fact that
most pairs do not usually settle down to family matters till mid-March.
It was therefore in the last days of that month that I first became acquainted with the crossbills of Breckland.

Breckland is a unique corner of England. It is characterized by the
'warren', a close-cropped, flint-strewn, rabbit-frequented flat, bordered
with long lines of Scots firs and sprinkled with copses, an occasional mere
and thicket of gorse. Here and there it is luxuriant in bracken, and to-day
much of it has been planted by the Forestry Commission. To an ornithologist it is famous chiefly as the locality in which the great bustard
made its last stand. To-day the place of the majestic bustard is taken by
the closely allied but smaller stone curlew, of which the Brecks are undoubtedly the headquarters, although it is by no means confined to
them. Here too breed woodlarks and nightjars, wheatears and lapwing,
and round the meres semi-feral Canada geese and ducks, even that rare
breeding bird, the gadwall. Yet the crossbills of the fir trees must be
regarded as the celebrities and the first attraction.

Crossbill nest-hunting is a pastime of very doubtful merits. Although
I had the valuable assistance of a friend in the Forestry Commission, his
help could go little further than obtaining the necessary permits to enter
certain areas controlled by the Commission. I found myself with a base,
a car and an Ordnance map—and Breckland to choose from. However,
that is the sort of problem I enjoy, for while every bird photographer is
at times indebted to others for nests, he who relies habitually on the discoveries of friends is not worthy of the title of bird photographer. Per-

sonal nest-finding should be a matter of his own pride, quite apart from the fact that only thereby will he really learn any field-knowledge of his subjects.

Now 'bird-nesting' is a scientific field sport. It is not, as is so popularly imagined, a game of peering tentatively and hopefully into hedgerows or trees on the 'hit or miss' principle of the schoolboy. In many species the nest is as good as found through the field glasses before it is ever looked for by the eyes. But some birds, particularly the smaller ones, do not always admit so scientific a method of discovery, and often, in the final stages at least, they call for the schoolboy technique of intensive search.

Amongst such must be numbered the crossbill. All I knew of the bird when I went to Breckland was its appearance, its call-note and that it nested in fir trees. I wandered casually down many lines of trees, all of which seemed very similar, hopeful of hearing the birds call—for the first step in nest-finding is clearly to locate your species. In point of fact I was not long in achieving this much success, for within an hour I heard several crossbills, only to find a family party in the tree tops, red male (what a lovely bird he is), greenfinch-like female and four streaked young, recently out of the nest and calling excitedly as they shivered their wings in the ecstatic anticipation of an offering of food from one or other of their parents.

This nest had clearly been one of the early ones. I began to wonder if perhaps after all most of the crossbills did nest in February. It was also clear that casual wandering down the lines of firs might lead to the over-looking of a pair which still had eggs, if I relied entirely on the call-note to attract my attention. With a family party it was a certain indication, for the chicks were never silent. But if a bird were merely incubating, there would not necessarily be any such advertisement, unless I was lucky enough to pass within ear-shot at the exact moment when the cock was approaching the hen with food.

My next line of attack therefore was to walk down the lines of firs, neck arched backwards and eyes inspecting the outstretching fir branches, for a sign of either nest or bird—the technique of the schoolboy in fact. I spent two whole days in this pursuit. Its amusement value is definitely over-rated. I finished with an extremely stiff neck and a headache from the glare of the sky and the hard work my eyes had put in examining fir branches. My notebook, however, as a result, if it could record no nest, at least profited, for I began to find crossbills, birds which, because they were silent, I should have undoubtedly overlooked otherwise.

During those two days I began to know the crossbill. I would find a pair in the tree tops and watch them. Although they led me to no nest, I saw something of their feeding methods. Parrot-like they sidle down a branch, with a very parrot-like gesture stoop forward and snip off a fir cone, carry it in their curved beaks to a substantial perch, transfer it to one foot, and proceed to extract the separate flakes and the seeds, discarding the cone when they have used but a small portion of it. There is clearly no rationing in the crossbill's world. A more deliberately wasteful species it would be difficult to find.

I came also to recognize signs of crossbill-working beneath the trees. Cones which have been attacked by them have the flakes nearest the stem removed or battered, while the bottom of the cone remains untouched. Here and there would be found cones, some of which had been eaten round like corn-cobs, the work probably of squirrels; others, perfect on one side, which on the other had been pulped by hammer-like blows, presumably by woodpeckers. Once, with a family party feeding above, I was peppered with rejected cones as though the crossbills were playful monkeys.

From time to time I located a solitary male bird which would encourage me to hope that he had an incubating mate close at hand to whom he would lead me. But neither intensive searching of the neighbouring trees nor patient watching of him ever produced a nest.

From watching many birds I saw also that there is no rule as to which way the beak is crossed. In some the lower mandible is twisted to the left, the upper to the right; in others it is the reverse. But this varies haphazardly, and it is not confined to sex. I wish now that I had taken statistical records of this point in the birds I watched. Later in a nest with newly hatched chicks I saw that the bill at birth is born straight, but fledglings out of the nest and in the tree tops accompanying their parents had bills already crossed, so that this development must occur early in life.

Persistence however brought its reward. Late in the evening of the third day, by which time I hesitate to think how many miles of 'neck-arching' I had done, I saw a female crossbill standing motionless beside a small greenfinch-like twig nest in a Scots fir, and not twenty feet up. I climbed up, a piece of disturbance to which the female paid not the least heed, for while I was digging my irons in, she went on to brood. Crossbills are famed for their fearlessness, and this individual was no exception. She allowed me almost to touch her before she scrambled reluctantly on to a side branch, exposing three eggs, indistinguishable from a greenfinch's. She herself was, except for her crossed beak and grey wings, also very like that bird, even to the yellow-green of her rump. When I sat back in a fork against the main stem, she returned to her eggs. The site was ideal: the bird tame. The quest seemed over.

On descending the tree I observed that my activities were an object of curiosity to a gentleman with field glasses, sitting in a stationary car on the main road. Crossbills being a great target of the egg-collectors—the species once figured as the star-turn of a famous prosecution—I decided to investigate. My observer proved to be another bird photographer, complete with camera, who was also looking for crossbills—or so he said. As it was by then growing dark, I told him that if he came to this spot the following morning, he could join me in photographing the crossbill.

I must have come down to earth in those days in the last shower of rain, for early the next morning there was no car at the pre-arranged place, nor was there any crossbill's nest. The bird was there, standing disconsolately on the site of its erstwhile nest, which had been removed along with the eggs. I may be doing an injustice, but if between dusk the night before and early morning of the next day another collector had found that nest, the coincidence was odd, especially as 'the photographer' of the night before never again materialized. I can only hope that the eggs have rotted in his cabinet.

It was a bad blow, and the prospect of more 'neck-arching' held little appeal. But the gods were kind and smiled on me, and before that day was out I had seen five more nests. One was in the same line of firs, at the very tip of the topmost branch, and to it I was attracted by the male. I passed beneath it at the very moment he was approaching with food. I heard his *jip-jip*, and looking up saw him feed the hen on the nest. It contained three eggs. The others were all in a small area of firs round a small farm. After tramping miles of similar country without success I came to the conclusion that crossbills form colonies of a sort, even if they are rather extended.

I did no climbing that day before I had first made sure that there were

PLATE 19. *Hobby at eyrie*

PLATE 21. *Hobby: a pause in feeding*

PLATE 20. *Hobby with chicks about 15 days old*

PLATE 22. *Young Hobbies exercising wings*

PLATE 23. *Young Hobbies about 28 days old*

PLATE 24. *Habitat of Hobby—The Plain*

PLATE 25. *Habitat of Hobby—The Heath*

PLATE 26. *Stone Curlew about to sit*

PLATE 27. *Stone Curlew hen taking over from cock*

PLATE 28. *Stone Curlew attempting to lure chicks away*

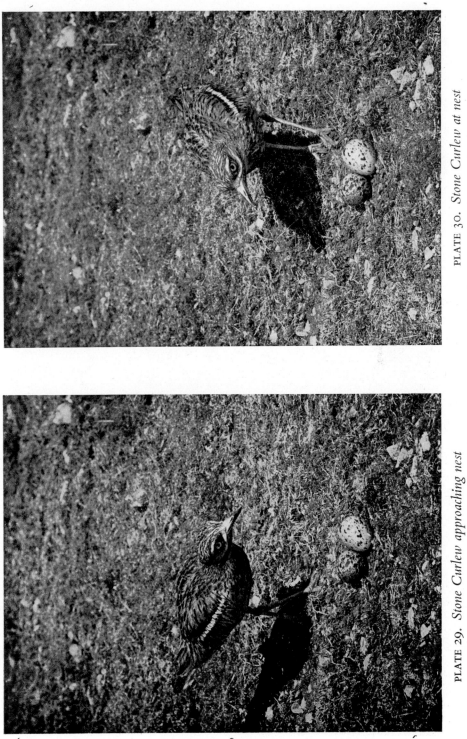

PLATE 30. *Stone Curlew at nest*

PLATE 29. *Stone Curlew approaching nest*

PLATE 31. *Dartford Warbler at nest*

no curious 'photographers' watching me, and, to make assurance doubly sure and having no mind for any further 'neck-arching', I sat beneath the nesting tree till dusk! The nuisance of the collector had already descended on me, and the number of trees, particularly in the neighbourhood of the small farm, which bore the marks of climbing irons was ready testimony of their activities. In fact nowhere else, except perhaps in the slightly similar country where the hobby breeds on Salisbury Plain, have I ever seen trees so scarred as in this part of Breckland.

The next morning I found one egg hatched and two chipping in the nest I had selected, and I breathed again with relief. Here I made my hide—the bird was not as tame as the first female and resented my unconcealed presence—and on April Fool's Day I was successful.

To complete the picture I drove from Breckland to Scotland and within a week I was watching the Scottish crossbill amongst the pines of Rothiemurchus. Had these northern birds heavier bills? In some specimens it certainly seemed to be the case, but by no means all. But a crossbill, be it Scottish or Continental, is still just a crossbill, a very delightful and colourful little parrot of the fir trees.

CHAPTER 3

Salisbury Plain

To the ordinary traveller Salisbury Plain does not always appeal as a beauty spot. Yet its wide open spaces of chalk with their scattered rings of trees, their lines of firs and clumps of ragged hawthorn and juniper possess a spaciousness that is often absent from the more typical pastoral country of the south. It is clean country, where the wind blows fresh, and where the great vault of the sky sweeps in front and behind unbroken, until it meets its horizon on the gentle slopes of the surrounding downs. And if these Wiltshire uplands fail to cast their spell upon the wanderer, he cannot fail to find his heart's desire in the luxuriant valleys of their crystal-clear rivers, rich in lush vegetation and big trout. For where the chalk stream takes its shining course is peace and contentment beyond measure—a land of sheer delight.

The valleys are, however, the province of the fisherman, himself here as an entomologist, a naturalist of note; for the angler who aspires to the trout of these waters will cast in vain if he has not learnt the story of the flies upon which his quarry feeds. The amazing life history of the *Ephemeridae*, however, fascinating though it is, is the province of the entomologist rather than of the bird-watcher. And although these same chalk valleys are rich in bird-life, it is on the downs above, on the sweeping chalk hills and in their clumps and lines of fir trees that he will find most to interest him.

This open country is the home of two species which, if they can hardly be said to be peculiar to it, are yet characteristic—the hobby and the stone curlew.

The hobby has every attribute of attraction. It has the appeal of

34

comparative rarity, an appeal which it is fashionable to deny, but which nevertheless holds a very real place in every bird-watcher's heart. It is handsome; it has the athlete's build. In fact, this small sickle-winged falcon, which can catch a swift in fair flight, is a glamorous bird personality.

Its fascination, however, has been its undoing, for there is surely no British bird so systematically harried by the egg-collecting fraternity. I hold no extreme views on this pursuit. I am indeed convinced that *much* of the damage attributed to collectors has been exaggerated beyond all reality, and it is patently clear that in many cases the cause of a species' rarity has been occasioned by other factors than egg-collecting. Above all, I pay tribute to the fine field-naturalists which this aspect of bird study has produced. Yet there is another side of the picture which eternally damns them—the ruthless harrying of certain species, either very rare or border-line cases, which would undoubtedly have a better chance of becoming common with the lack of their unhealthy attention. In the first category we have the phalarope and dotterel, species which will not stand *any* drain on their reproductive resources without endangering the species as a whole: in the second come a number, amongst which is the hobby.

Can it be denied that this grand falcon would be commoner than is at present the case if it were not thus harried? How indeed can it be otherwise? Many of the evil deeds of the egg-collector have been magnified in the telling, but it is difficult to exaggerate the concerted assault which is made against this bird every June on Salisbury Plain. Let the disbeliever go there for himself on the mid-Sunday of June. Few rings or clumps are without gentlemen with field glasses. If it is not every tree with a crow's nest in it that wears the scars of climbing irons, those without are in a very big minority. Nor indeed do the egg-men themselves attempt to deny it. They admit that the whole area is by some sort of jungle law parcelled out amongst a few of the 'king-pins' of the oology world. They will openly tell you that if you want to take a clutch of hobby on the Plain, the only safe method is to keep a few kestrel's eggs in your pocket, because it is necessary to take the hobby as it lays one by one, replacing each with a kestrel. If you do not adopt these tactics, a rival may well rush in and take your bird before she has laid her full set.

This scandalous state of affairs is not exaggerated. I live too close to the scene of operations not to be able to counter that line of attack, and as a photographer, anxious for the eggs to hatch to give me a chance, I have suffered too often under its system, and even if it is true that success with the hobby only came my way through the kindness and the help of an egg-collector (and I have many times been assisted by them in my work), yet the fact remains that the hobby raids are a disgrace, and a very shocking feature of British ornithology.

I know full well the old arguments, that hobbies, when robbed, regularly 'repeat'; that these second nests are left in peace and allowed to hatch; and that many first nests are not found on the fringes of the Plain. Be it so. Yet can any of them deny that the species would stand a better chance if it were left wholly in peace without having forcibly to delay its breeding season? It is a late-nesting bird in its normal routine, and young from these first eyries rarely fly before mid-August. It cannot help a migrant species to hold up the fledgling of its young for one month, till mid-September.

The arguments of the collectors are specious. The 'anti-hobby movement' is a poor one, a very poor one, and it is up to the chief participants to put an end to it, that the birds may be given every chance to prosper, and that others may enjoy the living feather and flesh and not the dead shell in cotton wool, which they are not even able to see.

The war should have given the hobby a chance, for many of its Salisbury Plain haunts have become gas experimental stations or ranges and training grounds. The 'No Admittance', which did not deter the peacetime collector for one moment, must under wartime security restrictions have kept many of the egg-thieves away for the last six years.

My own memories of the hobby are amongst the most vivid of my bird recollections. It is not a bird with which one comes into even momentary contact and then forgets, and although the field of my memories of this falcon covers many places both at home and abroad, sometimes at the nest, at others mere glimpses, all remain as clear to me now as at the time of their occurrence.

My first hobby I particularly remember, because contrary to the usual practice I saw the nest first and the bird afterwards. It was the last day of an Oxford term, and I was due to set out for Caithness and a very different type of bird life in the afternoon following. In the evening I got a report of a hobby about six miles away, and so with a companion rose early and bicycled out to the locality. It did not fit my textbook concep-

PLATE 33. *Dartford Warbler perched*

PLATE 32. *Dartford Warbler perched*

PLATE 34. *Nightjar approaching eggs*

PLATE 35. *Nightjar with newly-hatched chick*

tions of typical hobby ground, for it was an expanse of low country where a little tributary of the Thames ran through marshy country and pollarded willows. The hedgerows grew elms and an occasional oak, as they straggled about the valley. But there were no coniferous trees, and I had always been led to believe that the hobby was not found far from their association.

Since that day I have come to learn that, whilst in Wiltshire and Surrey firs are almost exclusively used for nesting, to the north of these strong-holds river valleys and marshy ground with scattered hedgerow trees, normally deciduous, are quite normal. Thus even on the Berkshire down-lands, where there is country available not at all unlike the Plain, there are as many pairs of hobbies in the river valleys as in the woods and copses of the upland chalk.

It should be noted that these lowland habitats are normally marshy, and for this the reason is not difficult to find. The hobby's food is two-fold, birds and insects. From my own experience it would appear that, although not exclusive in their tastes, individual pairs tend to specialize in one or the other type of food. Birds which favour river valleys are undoubtedly chiefly insectivorous, and clearly they select such a breed-ing haunt on account of the abundance of insect life, especially of dragon-flies, which emerges in these marshy spots during late summer.

By contrast, the upland and heath birds seem to prefer a diet of flesh. They will however quickly swing on to insects if the chance offers, and although I have never seen them do so, I have no doubt that they make periodical descents into the near-by chalk stream valleys to take toll of the bountiful insect life which those clear rivers produce.

That they quickly adopt an insect diet on the open Plain I once saw most vividly. I had run my car up a long valley to the edge of a wood, famous amongst the collectors for its hobbies, and I had walked far over the chalk, visiting the scattered clumps of pines in a vain effort to find an unrobbed nest. Two pairs of bereaved birds and scores of trees scarred with climbing irons had been my only reward. It was late when I got back to the car, and the stone curlews were already starting their eerie evening chorus. As though from nowhere, cockchafers began to hatch. They were buzzing everywhere, hitting me in the face and bump-ing into the windscreen of the car, a veritable cloud of locusts.

Gradually they got higher, and when they did so, I saw to my joy four hobbies enjoying the feast. They had appeared as from nowhere with that knowledge of natural phenomena which is ever noticeable in wild creatures, and which baffles all human explanation. The hatch had occurred with great suddenness. When it began, no hobbies were visible. Within five minutes there were four!

Until this moment I had always been slightly at a loss to reconcile with my own impression of this falcon its oft-quoted resemblance to a large swift. The unusually long wings naturally suggest this comparison, but until I watched the bird taking cockchafers, the likeness had never seemed very actual in life. But here as they alternately glided and flew over the valley, they were indeed very like big swifts. Lesser kestrels, also insectivorous, I have seen circling over a hill town in Andalucia in the evening and bearing a similar resemblance. Doubtless this type of 'hawking' calls for very similar tactics, which both the insect-eating falcons and the swifts know well and share in common.

Nevertheless I could not satisfy myself about the manner in which the hobbies were catching their prey. They were turning and twisting their heads from side to side, so that many chafers were doubtless caught directly by the mouth, but from time to time a bird would in an ungainly manner scratch its face whilst flying, but I was unable to see if in this process a chafer was being transferred to the mouth, having been previously caught in the talons. It was a great sight to watch, and I departed only with the fading light and the hobbies, when the chafers had spread abroad or gone to bed. My fisherman's mind could not help comparing it to a rise of trout, for at that very hour in the river not far away I knew that the trout in their element would be behaving in much the same way as the hobbies I had just watched in the sky, as the delicate female spinners of the blue-winged olive descended spent on to the water and drifted down the stream, a floating carpet of death.

On a stretch of country like Salisbury Plain nest-hunting for hobby is not in itself a difficult matter, for an ordnance map will mark all the possible clumps and rings of trees which suit this little falcon. Not that it is in fact quite as easy as that, for the hobby is not confined to the small, isolated wood, and the Plain country is not without extensive, sparsely grown woodlands of some size, in which a pair can easily hide themselves away. They will also readily use the long thin lines of firs which are such a feature of this part of Wiltshire. But energy and perseverance will bring its reward—with one big proviso, so long as the egg-collectors have not been there beforehand. How lugubrious and infuriating a business this can be I know well, but thorough as is their work, nests are missed, even in the best-known localities.

In this connection I remember early in one August visiting the Plain on a hobby hunt. I have long since ceased to compete in the June mêlée. I now wait till the egg-men have finished falling over themselves, and I go my rounds in late July or early August, looking for the second attempts at rearing a family. It is a pleasant annual expedition, for the breeding season is over and finished for the great majority of birds, and it is good indeed to have so fine a species as hobby to pursue when all else has little to offer. The little copses, deep in willow herb, are then at their best.

On one such evening a friend rang me up to say that he had located a hobby in suspicious circumstances near a small wood which occupies a conspicuous place on a collector's marked map. I have frequently seen birds near it, but without exception they had always been bereaved. However, by early August the second nest should have been nearly a month old and with eggs almost hatching, for the hobby takes about three weeks to 'repeat' if its first clutch is taken.

The next morning we accordingly ran the car over the chalk, bumping across the rabbit warrens to the small wood on top of the down. It was arranged that my companion should drive round to the far side and hoot, whilst I stayed on the other to watch events.

At his road-hog's signal wood pigeons swarmed forth, like rock-doves out of a sea cave when startled by a shot. They came out in all directions, and I was beginning to wonder if I should ever see a hobby, if indeed there was one, amongst them. Hardly had the thought crossed my mind when a falcon came tearing through the tall Scots firs and sped away over the chalk at a speed which made the cushats look very amateur fliers.

We plunged into the undergrowth, in August so luxuriant that the nettles in places will sting your chin, and surveyed a forest of scattered firs, the great majority of which held an old crow's nest. The day was hot: the trees were very tall and quite branchless for some forty feet, and the prospect of finding the occupied eyrie by the process of elimination did not appeal in the very least. We therefore sat down to wait for the falcon's return. When an hour produced no sign of her, I began to wonder if she was indeed nesting in this wood, and took another stroll round the possible nesting trees. Suddenly I caught sight of some 'whitewash' on a branch near an old crow's nest at the top of the tallest and most

branchless Scotsman in all that wood. It was a sufficient clue, for all raptorial chicks from the very earliest age practise nest-sanitation by
evacuating the liquid faeces over the edge of the nest. The climb was
wearisome, but I was overjoyed at the end of it to see three lusty chicks
of about two weeks old in the nest, white balls of indignant fury.

It was indeed a surprise, for this was obviously a first laying. No
'repeat' could by the 3rd of August be so advanced as to have chicks as
old as a fortnight. It is just possible that the first nest had been particularly early, but it is more likely that it had been slightly on the late side,
and that as a consequence it had missed the main invasion of the egg-
men during the first three weeks of June.

Be that as it may, here was a hobby *hatched* in one of the best-known
breeding woods. I took my hat off to that bird! Outside the big, straggling woods and on the edge of the Plain it is the only pair I have ever
had reason to believe get away with their first attempt, for these isolated
copses, so beloved of this bird, are too well known and too easy to comb
out thoroughly.

That August day was a red-letter one in the annals of my hobby
experiences, for it is the only one on which I have found two occupied
eyries on the same day. We worked a number of regular hobby sites
without so much as seeing a bird, breeding woods which I knew that
very year had been occupied by nesting pairs which had as usual been
robbed. Never a sign of the falcons did we find. Does the hobby *always*
repeat? The collectors in self-defence will maintain that it does so, but I
have so often drawn a blank in localities where I know a pair have been
robbed of their first laying without seeing any evidence of a second nest
that I wonder very much if all do make another effort. Some, however,
certainly do, for on this day we came eventually to a rookery where a
pair of hobbies regularly resort for their first nest, and I knew that in this
year they had been robbed in June of their first clutch.

The rookery was in a long line of mixed fir and beech trees, set in a
very steep valley, ideal for observation in that the sides rose so precipit-
ously, for chalk hills, that the top of the rooks' nests could be inspected
with ease through field glasses. About a mile down the valley the line of
trees did a sudden left-hand bend and, deserting the low ground, ran
uphill over the chalk down.

As we were approaching this corner, at the point where the rooks'
nests were most dense in both fir and beech trees, a falcon came tearing

over, calling loudly with that shrill alarm cry which is common to all species of the family. If it had been difficult to find the occupied tree in the first copse of the day, it was a hundred-fold more difficult in the large rookery in which we now found ourselves. Nests were festooned in the branches above. The steep hillside, however, afforded an excellent vantage point for observation, and thither we went, and concealing ourselves in the shade of an elder, sat down to watch. The falcon was quieter by now and high up in the sky, flying with rapid wing beats alternated by long glides, at times almost soaring.

These antics brought her mate on to the scene. He came from afar and at a great height. As she climbed to meet him, he made a stupendous dive, taking many hundreds of feet of sunlight in the twinkling of an eye, a lovely sight and one of those supreme moments in a bird-watcher's history. They played together high up for a little while. Then suddenly both birds stooped towards the trees, the male throwing up again as he reached their level, but the falcon came swishing past us and landed amidst a pile of rooks' nests. She was a superb streak of animation as she swept in with the sun full on her. Everything glistened, her blue-black back, the rich red of her thighs, the boldly streaked breast, and her black moustaches, clear cut against the white of her face.

That was a memorable day, but it cannot rank as high as the time when I sat in a hide within fifteen feet of the hobby at the nest. That year I had toiled hard for success. The Plain had revealed many birds, but never an occupied eyrie suitable for photography. I heard from a friend of a nest not twenty miles from Hyde Park Corner. He was not a photographer and, not knowing the conditions required, was not prepared to say if it would suit my purpose. But a hobby's eyrie occupied was not to be ignored, and I motored up to inspect.

The hobby has three main habitats—the isolated clump, typical of Salisbury Plain, the wide river valley of the South Midlands, and the open heath with straggling fir woods and lone trees, typical of the Surrey and Hampshire 'commons'. To these there may be added normal woodland, and I am convinced that more pairs nest in this type of country than is often realized. In it they can be very inconspicuous and difficult to track down. There is a pair within three miles of my house which annually I see for short glimpses throughout the summer, and which certainly breed. But I have never succeeded in finding their eyrie in the many, many stretches of woodland which carpet this vale. In the evening from time to time the pair will circle over the woods at the edge of the near-by common, now over one copse, now over another, rarely twice in the same place. Early in the season I see the courtship pursuit over the tree tops, the male chasing the falcon at full speed and both birds calling loudly and excitedly. But find their nest I cannot. There is too much suitable ground, all equally good to a hobby's eye and tastes.

This new nest brought me into immediate acquaintance with the heath habitat. Here hobby nest-hunting is a very, very difficult business. For the most part it is impossible to sit down and watch the birds until they give some clue to their secret. Tree to tree searching is the only method, but where there are hundreds of trees, and a large percentage with old crows' nests in their branches, there is a big margin for error. A complete comb-out is more easily said than done.

The nest-tree, when reached, was a tall Scots fir, much like many a one we had passed *en route*. There was nothing to indicate tenancy, for no hobby circled excitedly round. When I had climbed about forty feet without a sign, I began to have serious misgivings, which were not relieved until I was within a foot of the nest. Then with a swish and a steep dive the falcon flashed away, twisting between the trees. The nest contained two eggs, typical of the species, lighter than a kestrel's and looking as though they had been sprinkled with dark brown out of a pepper pot.

This eyrie was not ideal for close observation and tree hide construction, but a week later I received tidings of another containing two young about five days old and one addled egg. This was in very similar country —wide heath with dense fir woods, although the trees were nothing like so tall as in the previous habitat. The eyrie was, as usual, an old carrion crow's nest, about twenty feet up a ridiculously small sapling pine, and if the site presented many problems, I was weary of finding hobbies' nests and yet never attaining my age-old desire of sitting within a few feet of this beautiful little falcon. Therefore, although it was obvious that my perch would be precarious and uncomfortable to a degree, I moved in to the local inn and set to work.

When finally the hide was built, the eyasses were about a fortnight old, charming little balls of white down, most intolerant of examination, lying on their backs and lashing out with their talons at the intruder's hand.

During my frequent visits to the nesting tree in these preliminary stages the parents were disappointingly undemonstrative. Hobbies are credited with striking an intruder, in much the same way as a great skua will strike an enemy near its nest. But this pair never tried any form of intimidation for some time. In fact, they were conspicuously absent when I was at the nest or up the tree in which my hide was being built.

On the first day on which I started photography, however, a big change came over the demeanour of the falcon. She now no longer made herself scarce in the surrounding timber, but mobbed us incessantly as we crossed the heathery glade which separated the main wood from the sentinel outposts of sapling firs which fringed it and in which the nest was placed. Her attacks were most menacing, tremendous stoops from a great height with half-closed wings, which only opened out when the bird was within a few feet of the head. Throughout the attacks she kept up an incessant *kee-kee*-ing, which undoubtedly made her performance more frightening. It was a glorious display of courage and determination, according well with the plucky character of the bird.

What occasioned this sudden change of behaviour from bashful and sient effacement to dashing and vociferous attack I find difficult to assess. No bird's mind is capable of reasoning that until the game is definitely up, a policy of retirement gives less away than one of suspicious observation or of open resentment. Yet why did this particular falcon vanish into thin air for the first few days and then, making a complete *volte-face*, adopt the entirely opposite tactics of open attack? The attacking stage started when the young were estimated to be fifteen days old, and they undoubtedly increased in ferocity until on the twenty-eighth day the chicks flew. Although the nearer *adult* young birds become, the weaker grows the family tie until finally they part company completely, I have often noticed that the nearer they are to being fully *fledged*, the more anxious bird parents seem to grow for their safety.

That the hobby, however, is not demonstrative when the nest is first found—and that in my experience is the rule—has its advantages. In my own pair, at least, the policy of self-effacement saved the bird's life, for between my first inspection of the nest and the beginning of my operations a very well-made hide had appeared at the foot of the tree. I could guess its purpose, and a visit to the head keeper confirmed that it was indeed intended for the destruction of the hobbies. He listened to my entreaties, and I did all in my power to convince him for the future that the hobby was harmless to game. I hope and pray it did not all fall on deaf ears, for that stretch of heath and woodland regularly harbours breeding pairs.

His reason for willing the bird's destruction did not augur well for the future. He *thought* it was a kestrel, and as such he also *thought* it would be healthier dead than alive. Just like that. So easy, so childish, so selfish! It makes one cry. Heaven knows, you will look far to find anyone who more dearly loves a shot at a pheasant or a partridge than myself, but if the privilege of doing so is only to be obtained by the crass idiocy of shooting everything with a hooked beak, without even bothering to identify the species, let alone really knowing something about its food, then I will gladly pack up my gun for all time. It is the utter selfishness of it all that reduces me to open rage, and the blame must rest with the landowner. The keeper is a servant; he has his bread and butter to consider, and if 'birds' do not show up well, a full 'larder' of vermin corpses is useful visible evidence that he has been on the job. It matters not that a high percentage of the victims are innocent. Only the man who deserves to own land, one who cherishes its every aspect, can correct this state of affairs. Let him draw up a 'black list' of vermin, founded on fair play and a fair consideration of known facts, and let his keepers obey. There are many fine keepers, but there are a multitude of very ignorant onces. Menaced by the collector, menaced by the keeper, menaced by all who would disturb it (which includes myself!), what a life is the hobby's! But I am proud to have saved the life of one pair and of their two chicks.

By the time my observations started the parents had ceased to take any interest in their chicks except to feed them. All the raptorial birds with which I have had dealings are extremely Spartan towards their young as soon as their down affords them sufficient warmth. Between feeds the falcon sat at the very top of a neighbouring fir and preened herself whilst the young slept. This practice was very reasonable when the sun shone. But there came a period of torrential rain and thunderstorm, when the eyasses were so drenched that I very nearly produced a hot-water bottle. Yet during this very bad twenty-four hours she herself took cover, but left her soaking chicks to their own devices. She was not in the least afraid of the hide, and I grew furious with her as I sat anxiously in cover a hundred yards away and prayed that she would do her duty, for her seeming callousness made me fear for the chicks. But the top of her sentinel post was good enough for her, and except to feed and at night,

PLATE 36. *Nightjar: unsuspicious and eye wide-open*

PLATE 37. *Nightjar: suspicious and eye closing*

PLATE 38. *Nightjar: 'protective' position along perch*

PLATE 39. *Nightjar: full crouching position, eye a mere slit*

the eyasses were left to look after themselves in blinding rain and thunderstorm.

When the young were about a fortnight old, feeding occurred at intervals of from two and a half to three hours. So far as my evidence went, the male bore the full brunt of bread-winning, whilst his mate played the idle role of sentry on her fir. I could see her from my hide, silhouetted against the sky, her slim and neat shape clear-cut. Her off-spring apparently occasioned her no worry, for I never saw her con-sciously so much as glance at them: her chief concern and pastime was her personal toilet, and I must agree that on her periodic visits to the nest her plumage did justice to her efforts. It was always immaculate.

The lazy hours of high-perched sentry duty were relieved only at feed-ing time. Of this all of us, the falcon, her chicks and myself, got advance warning. The male's advent was heralded by a very soft, plaintive, almost nasal, call, *kee-ë-kee-ë kee-ë*, repeated seven or eight times. It was in no sense like the alarm note, although thus syllabized it may appear so, but it lacked all the harshness of the call of the agitated and anxious bird. It was the signal for all of us. I glued my eyes to every peep-hole; the eyasses began to squeak; the lazy falcon straightened out as though a spring had shot through her. Then occurred a 'pass', the speed of which was most inspiring. The male came over the nesting trees like a streak of winged lightning. As he did so, the same spring which had shot through the falcon sent her like a bullet from her perch. As she rose to meet her lord, he towered, and as he towered, she closed with him momentarily. Then they parted, he to his business and she to dive like a comet for the nest. It was a truly wonderful exhibition of flying, and I never hope to see anything better.

At the age of a fortnight the eyasses were still being fed directly by their parent, and feeds lasted as long as ten minutes, the falcon tearing at the bird (which she brought to the nest in her talons) and offering the morsels to her impatient youngsters, who kept up an incessant squeaking all the time and were obviously disappointed when there was no more.

Unfortunately I could not watch this nest for the remaining fortnight of its habitation, and when I next met the chicks, they were about twenty-eight days old and ready to fly. A great change had come over the balls of white down which I had last left. They were now miniature editions of their parents. On the back and wings they were brown rather than slate, and tips of all the feathers were emarginated with buff, whilst the streaking of the breast was less clearly defined than in the adult, and the ground colour was buff not white. Much of their time was spent in wing exercises and preening. The latter gave me some amusement, for the youngsters nearly choked themselves with the soft down which was now moulting rapidly. When flapping and stretching their wings, they exposed a very pretty mottling of black on cream.

I shall not readily forget this last day with my hobby, for although on it I got only one visit from the adult, it was heralded by a magnificent 'pass', and as she alit at the nest for a moment to deposit the food, I got a photograph which I prize above all my other negatives, of the falcon with her two fully fledged chicks.

When she had gone, I gave the eyasses a little time to devour their meal, and then climbed up to inspect the food. As I did so, the chicks spread their wings and flew for the first time. The prey was a swift. I dearly wished I could have seen the male catch it.

Although we have wandered from the Plain to the heath, the hobby is for me essentially a bird of the open chalk with its scattered clumps of trees. Of these it is by no means the only bird of prey, for it shares them with numerous kestrels and odd pairs of sparrow hawks, though the latter undoubtedly prefer the bigger woods of the valley. Nevertheless, I have found them noticeably partial to a small clump, not only on the Plain but also on the Sussex and Berkshire Downs.

The rabbit-cropped, chalk-scarred levels and valleys are the province of a restricted bird population. Skylarks soar and sing over them as blithely as over the lush meadows of the low ground, and smart wheat-ears clack with alarm, their tails bobbing in their concern, and nest in the many rabbit burrows. But the bird of this coverless land is the stone curlew.

I went to school with the stone curlew, or at least near it, and as it was the first nest I ever found of a species which might legitimately be deemed uncommon, it occupies a privileged place in my personal memories. Well it might, for I have sat in hides over no less than six different pairs, and watched from each that cautious and stealthy approach to the eggs which is so characteristic of the bird.

The stone curlew is for me at its best as a voice of the gloaming. How often, as I have returned from fishing the evening rise or, it may be, from a long day on the Plain, have I heard the curlew's nightly chorus! It begins with the witching hour when the sun is down but the light not yet quite gone, the hour when the elder shrubs and juniper bushes seem to take on uncanny shapes of things that do not appear in the hard light of day. Then from one side of the valley the quiet *cour-lee* steals forth, to be taken up afar by another bird out upon its evening business. Then another, further off, takes up the theme: then perhaps another, quite close by. It is a restrained and eerie concert, but it fits the furtive birds that make it, and without it the valleys and downs would lose much of their charm. Perhaps I remember it best in another clime, on an April night in Andalucia, when a full moon lit up the desolate waste of sun-dried Spanish *marismas* and the parklike country of the Coto Doñana on their verge. It was a night of utter stillness, and all round in the scrub the stone curlews were busy at their part-singing. And I have thus heard it on the equally desolate Camargue and on another Plain, the legendary Plain of Hercules, La Crau, that wilderness of stones and mirage that stretches between Arles and Marseille.

By day the stone curlew is, like the nightjar or the owls, and with equal reason, an inactive bird. Its large yellow eye bears eloquent testimony to its crepuscular and nocturnal way of life. If you see it by daylight, you will see a long-legged, brown-streaked plover, running rapidly over the skyline, or making for scanty juniper cover. You will not easily make it fly, unless the ground is very flat, for the stone curlew on the wing shows much white, and the bird believes in the maxim of out of sight, out of mind.

Perhaps occasionally you may see it at its courting—a very stiff and correct performance, as the cock bird walks sedately by his lady with tail almost erect, making full use of the black band underneath and with head held low to the ground. Every now and then he will break off in the middle of his display and start feeding. Then, as if suddenly remembering his business, he runs rapidly back and waltzes round the lady of his choice. From time to time he will lower himself like a lapwing and with breast on the ground and tail high form a 'scrape', an apology of a nest, his suggestive love-offering.

He is not easily thus surprised. Of the vigilance of an incubating stone curlew, even though its eyes be closed, I have had much evidence. The head and shoulders of a man a mile away are all the warning required, and without more ado the eggs are left to the mercy of their remarkable protective coloration. As so often, a car gives no cause for alarm, and I have driven over the chalk to within a few yards of the incubating bird.

At the nest, once they reach it—and wondrous cautious is the approach—they are unexciting birds. Drowsiness quickly seizes them, and it is only when the male comes to change places, or when the eggs are hatching that there is any real activity. The few change-overs which I have been fortunate enough to witness have produced no ceremony or display. In all cases one bird has left the eggs whilst the other has been a few yards away, and except for a sort of crooning conversation in very low tones that has been the end of the incident.

At a nest with newly hatched chicks, however, I saw a pair of lethargic, sleepy stone curlews galvanized into feverish paroxysms of anguish. My hide had for many days been over a nest with eggs, and the birds had lost all fear of it. On arrival one day I found the eggs hatched and the two chicks about twenty yards away. I accordingly shifted the hide to their new site, confidently expecting that the two babes would rise and run off as soon as their parents appeared on the scene. In due course both birds came hastily towards their offspring, 'grunting' loudly. One then approached nearer, and, with brooding patch exposed and all fluffed out, sat within a few inches of the chicks, getting up and flopping down repeatedly and calling quietly with the clear intent of luring them away from the menacing erection of canvas which had so unaccountably walked from its original position.

When this device failed to produce the desired result, both birds started an extraordinary display, directed apparently against the hide and not the human presence. It first took the form of a much quickened performance of the courtship walk, the head low and the wings outstretched, but the gait was not sedate but very rapid. When this failed to have any effect, one bird, the hen, I think, made several excited little jumps into the air, falling after each prone on its breast with wings outstretched over the flints of the down. This was attended by a curious hissing note, quite unlike anything I have ever heard before from a stone curlew, but very similar to an explosion of indignation to which I once heard a woodcock give utterance when I took her photograph as she incubated eggs. The performance itself was paralleled in my experience by that of a nightjar in a similar plight, which in like manner thus leapt into the air, falling prone with wings full stretched.

This behaviour greatly interested me. In its last stages it comes into the category of 'injury-feigning'. Now, while all bird-watchers are familiar with this practice in the face of the actual human presence or of

48

PLATE 40. *Woodlark*

PLATE 41. *Woodlark, showing eye-stripe and stumpy tail*

PLATE 42. *Skylark with chicks*

PLATE 43. *Nightingale*

PLATE 51. *Nuthatch*

PLATE 50. *Greater Spotted Woodpecker*

a natural enemy, this is the first occasion on which I have seen it employed against an inanimate object, in this case, a canvas hide. That the bird did not *consciously* know that the hide contained a human being must surely be taken for granted. Otherwise, why, when it only had eggs, had it accepted it without grave suspicion, and why, when the eggs had hatched, run over the top of the down and out of sight when I was there in flesh and blood, and yet come up within a few yards when only the hide was there?

It is to be noted that 'injury-feigning' is the last expedient to which resort was made in the bird's anxiety. First of all comes quite normal action in the face of danger—a hurried return to the vicinity of the chicks—natural, when danger had been near; then an attempt to lure them away; when that does not succeed, courtship gestures follow; and finally, a display of 'injury-feigning', directed against the hide.

The interpretation and the understanding of bird display have of late become subjects to which serious ornithologists have given considerable attention. The most reasonable explanation so far advanced to account for such behaviour as that of the stone curlews now under consideration is that 'emotion' in a bird's world is released by two main instincts, self-preservation and reproduction, and that when either the bird itself or its chicks are threatened, a 'behaviour-pattern' comes into play. When normality breaks down, when there is conflict of instincts, or when a bird is thwarted in the expression of its normal routine, resort is made, as an outlet, to a set train of behaviour in which the actions are associated alike with the two vital drives of its life—the need to preserve itself and the need to reproduce itself.

In the light of this theory, look again at the stone curlew's behaviour. Its first reactions are quite normal. It runs over the down and out of sight. It returns hurriedly to the neighbourhood of its chicks as soon as the coast is clear. On arrival, however, it finds that the hide which had previously been some distance away is now very close to the object of its anxiety, its young, the object of one of its main drives in life, reproduction. Its instinct is to brood them. It is thwarted because the hide has introduced something it does not understand, of which it is perhaps afraid. There is a conflict of its 'emotions'. It wants to brood (reproduction), yet it wants to run away (self-preservation). It tries a compromise —to lure the chicks off. When that fails, its 'emotions' overflow, and a behaviour-pattern follows in which the actions are partly those of courtship, partly of 'injury-feigning'—a confused, almost irrational, jumble of gestures both coming from a common origin, the need to continue the race. Hence display to a mere hide, because it was thwarting its normal behaviour.

The introduction of actions normally associated with courtship is a not uncommon feature of bird display at such times of great stress and strain. I have seen exactly the same thing in a pair of black-throated divers desperately anxious for the safety of their chick which I had caught on the bank of their breeding loch. If we accept the theory that 'emotion' in a bird springs from one common origin of two instincts, self-preservation and reproduction, then the confusion of courtship gestures with 'injury-feigning', although the two reasons for their release are so different, at least becomes understandable.

CHAPTER 4

Dorset Heathland

Dorset, the county of my adoption, has few rivals amongst all the shires for the variety and loveliness, and, above all, the unspoilt tranquillity of its countryside. Within its small confines the proud possessor of chalk downs and fertile vale, open heath and tall cliffs, luxuriant river valleys and sand-dunes, marsh and rich woodland, it can satisfy all moods, save that which demands a mountain. For ten years now within its boundaries I have done my daily birding, and right deep is my debt to Dorset. Yet in the midst of all this variety I have always enjoyed most my days on her heaths, for they are wild heaths and spacious, and on them a man may escape from his fellows and have only the wind for company. It is true that there is much which the very necessary exercising of tanks has spoilt; but there is still much whereon it is not very difficult to get lost amongst heather and pine trees. Within a few miles of towns of the size of Bournemouth and Poole are places where only scattered firs grow out of acres of gorse and ling, where curlews cry, and where perhaps even a handsome cock Montagu's harrier passes at his hunting. The car may be parked but two miles away on a big modern road that in twenty minutes will take you into thronging life: yet here for a brief space is a peace, almost a remoteness, that is as refreshing as it is surprising. And for the ornithologist is the added joy that a short journey can transfer him into a world of different birds. I never hear the curlew on these Dorset heaths without being transported by the noise to moors and fells that are many, many miles away.

Yet, though for me the curlew is always the surprise note of these heaths, as indeed it is also of the Surrey 'commons', my wanderings amongst the gorse and heather have in the main had for their object the pursuit of smaller quarry. For in these surroundings the local and most attractive Dartford warbler makes its home. It is my good fortune that within half an hour's run in the car from my house all twelve of the British breeding warblers may be found nesting. For ten of them I have no need to walk more than three miles, and in certain seasons, to bring the total to eleven, a pair of marsh warblers breed within that distance. But for the Dartford I have always to visit the heath.

Apart from its rarity and its unique place as our only non-migratory member of its family, the Dartford warbler is in itself a most engaging little bird, yet one which it is not easy to see, even on ground which is well-populated. It is a great skulker, a bird one glimpses rather than watches, a voice in the undergrowth, only seldom perching for long within unobstructed view. And on certain days, particularly wild and windy ones, when the gorse and heather that are its delight toss and sway, you will cross a heath which you know holds Dartfords and see never so much as a sign of one, until it seems they have all departed elsewhere. Yet on the very next day, should it be still and sunny, as you cross the very same ground, they will surprise you by appearing on all sides, suddenly from the depths of a gorse bush throwing themselves into the air in that abandoned little song flight which is typical of both it and its common relative, the whitethroat. Equally suddenly they vanish from sight, but perhaps occasionally perching in full view on top of a bush.

It is at such favoured moments, usually on a warm early spring morning, that the Dartford warbler is at its best. On such days it leaves behind a very clear-cut impression—of a tiny wee mite of a bird with a very long and high-cocked tail, standing on the very tipmost top of the yellow flowers of a gorse sprig, then quickly diving into cover, to reappear yards away from its vanishing point.

From my many days in the company of Dartfords I have always come away with this same typical impression. I have seen them on the Surrey 'commons' and the Dorset heaths, amongst the cistus of an Andalucian sierra, in the scrub of the Coto Doñana and amongst the dwarf gorse of Provençal hills. Though the sub-species may have differed with locality, from each I retain the same picture of the Dartford, the same little long-tailed bird perched momentarily on a sprig of scrub and diving hurriedly

PLATE 53. *Green Woodpecker and chick*

PLATE 52. *Green Woodpecker near nest-hole*

PLATE 54. *Sparrow Hawk feeding chicks*

into cover, as though the light of open day was too bright for it.

The Dartford warbler however well repays the minor irritations involved in getting a satisfactory view of it, for if casual glimpses indicate a rather dull, dowdy bird, a close inspection quickly shows how false that impression is. It is not a colourful bird; but there is a delightful subtlety about the pink shade of its underparts, and the throat is attractively flecked with white. Its head feathers it can raise in such a way as to form almost a crest, and indeed it frequently does so. But its chief feature is its long tail which at all times forms the readiest clue to its identity. Seen in flight as it trails behind, it seems almost an embarrassment, too great a load for the small wings to manage.

There are two main opportunities of seeing the Dartford warbler at its best—in the early morning and at the nest. Dawn is an ornithologist's happy hunting time. All birds are most active at that hour, and none more so than the warbler family. Then they court and feed, sing and build their nests with a vigour that at a later hour has lost much of its initial gusto. I remember particularly one morning in the Alpilles in Provence when the Dartford—and with them Sardinian and subalpine —warblers went mad with joy. The cistus scrub that by mid-day became lifeless was at daybreak alive with singing warblers. I have never anywhere since seen Dartfords behave like it. They were in transports of joy, throwing themselves into the air and boomeranging back to their perches. Although I sought for bigger quarry in the form of Egyptian vulture, the little birds seemed determined that they should not escape notice, in an almost aggressive manner forcing themselves upon my attention.

At the nest they can be delightfully tame, and it is then, as always, that they may be seen and watched to best advantage. At first all you will hear will be the harsh scolding note from the undergrowth, with never a sign of the bird that makes it. But if you keep still, curiosity—or anxiety—will prevail, and upon a gorse perch it will fly, still scolding and still twitching its long tail nervously. Be patient still longer, and you will find the chicks fed within a few feet. At one nest in Dorset right by a main road the hen bird actually brought food to her chicks on one side of the nest, whilst I was with my hand arranging the gorse on the other, prior to taking photographs.

Now that Montagu's harrier has become so rare on the Dorset heaths, the Dartford warbler is undoubtedly their chief claim to ornithological importance. Yet many other species share these rolling slopes of heather and pine. From time to time even crossbills nest: a few pairs of hobby falcons do so annually, as also an occasional long-eared owl. A single pair of tree-nesting ravens are perhaps the avian celebrities. In the straggling hawthorns of the valleys red-backed shrikes nest in common with many yellow hammers, while smart stonechats and the ubiquitous meadow pipit and skylark are the common small birds of the open heather. Amongst the last, if you search hard, woodlarks may be found.

There are few British species more overlooked than the woodlark. It belongs to that group of small brown birds which are the despair of many an aspiring ornithologist, and which are only sought for and identified by the more experienced and more enthusiastic bird watchers. Its superficial resemblance to the common, well-known skylark only adds to its nonentity. Yet it is not a difficult bird to identify. The comparison of coloured plates of the two species might not seem very helpful; the two best diagnostic characters, the light and conspicuous eye-stripes meeting on the nape to form a band, and the short stumpy tail, do not encourage you to feel that the bird in the field wears an identity disc round its neck. And indeed you will not best find your first woodlark by plumage distinctions. In point of fact, when you see it well, the light eye-stripe is very noticeably broader than the skylark's, and the mottling of the whole plumage has been painted with more contrast between the different shades of brown. But neither of these points is likely first to locate the bird for you. I think I can truthfully say that I have seen and found every single woodlark of my experience by either its song or its appearance in flight.

The song, being elaborate, defies a description that is based on mere human syllables. Its musical quality is exceptional, for its notes have a very sweet and liquid timbre. Whilst obviously lark-like, it is at the same time quite distinct from the skylark's much-praised outpourings of joy. In the flight from which it is delivered the woodlark travels over a greater area of country, planing with quivering wings over its territory, and normally descending in a rapid dive on to a tree or bush rather than to the ground itself. The skylark, on the other hand, apart from finishing normally in the grass, rises in spirals to a definite 'pitch' and does not roam far while at its singing. I cannot imagine anyone who is out for birds and with his ears alert meeting so fine a song and not pressing the matter further. Once attention is drawn, the rest is easy.

Dorset Heathland

Though the song provides a ready clue to identification, the wood-lark is a spasmodic singer even at the height of the season. It rarely in my experience pours forth the unceasing strains which are the skylark's great contribution to the volume of spring bird music. Reliance on song alone may bring disappointment—or at least delay. I have sat in April on ground which I knew was frequented by woodlarks and yet never heard the cock bird give tongue, although he has been perched on guard all the time on a near-by bush. As a result I find most of my woodlarks by plodding over likely ground and disturbing the birds. For, when flushed, they have an unbalanced shape and weak flight. The stumpy tail gives a poor impression at most angles, but on the wing it is very conspicuous. The wings seem over-large for the bird and the flight has all the undula-tions of a green woodpecker's. Seen directly overhead, the tail indeed is so short that it looks as though it had been moulted or broken off short.

The identification of birds by such slender means, such mere impres-sions, as this is frequent. It has been called the 'jizz' of a bird, some in-definable character of shape or flight or attitude, which to the experi-enced and seeing eye gives the main clue to ultimate identification. Birds are so rarely seen in the field in the perfection in which they are portrayed by bird-artists that plumage distinctions, unless the pattern is very strik-ing, often fail to provide a practical answer—for the excellent reason that the bird in question does not parade them for critical scrutiny through the field glasses. 'Jizz', that vague something about the carriage, outline, gait or demeanour of a bird, will often tell a clearer tale than colour and markings. The woodlark's stumpy appearance, coupled with its dipping flight, is an excellent example.

The typical woodlark haunt is not easy to describe. In Dorset it is mainly a bird of the heath as it is in Suffolk, but it breeds also on rough commons and hillsides. In Devon it is a bird of the bracken-strewn coombs. In the Cotswolds it delights in the rough grass of the downs, especially where the most meagre, low-growing brambles strew the ground. This type of haunt is one difficult to paint in words, but which experience soon teaches. Recently, in Essex, a county where the species is not supposed now to breed, I was obliged to exercise my dog over a small bit of rough ground of birch and oak scrub, with clearings of broom and very poor bramble. It was so much a facsimile of the very first woodlark breeding haunt I ever saw—in the Cotswolds—that even in mid-winter I could not help thinking it exactly suited to this lark, despite the fact that it is not supposed to breed in the neighbourhood. Great then was my joy in March to hear a woodlark's song, and in April to find a nest—the first record for Essex for many years. But always the typical breeding grounds are extensive.

On such ground, where the possible nesting sites have no limits, and where often large areas are equally suitable, the finding of a woodlark's nest is a matter of no small difficulty. Casual, even systematic, quartering of the ground will pay a poor dividend, unless luck is heavily weighted on your side. Indeed, all bird-nesting which relies merely on chance appeals but little to me. By waiting or listening or watching you see and learn and get to know your bird, and the likelihood of your finding its secret is greater.

Woodlark nest-hunting is indeed an athletic sport unto itself. There are two chief methods, the one as lethargic as the other is energetic. The female on the nest seems to feed twice a day, in the morning and in the evening. By watching the cock bird then you may in time see him fly down to the ground and join his mate. Usually after a few preliminary mouthfuls near the nest he will take her further afield, as though a little exercise were as necessary to her well-being as a little food. She will not be away long. Watch her carefully as she returns, for it is now that she will give her nest away. Within a small area near where she pitches will be her secret.

The energetic method is less restful and far more exhausting. The chief requirement is a good physical wind. Find your cock bird and chase him, quite literally chase him. Run after him, give him no peace, and in due course (you may be very hot before he obliges) he will call his lady off her nest. The rest is easy, for it but remains to take cover and watch her return, which she will do quickly enough once the coast is clear.

Woodlarks vary considerably in their response to this treatment. Some males will oblige in a few minutes: others will make you wonder if they are ever going to play. But in the end you will get your reward, although by that time your coat and collar and tie and all superfluous garments may have been shed.

For myself I find a combination of the two methods best. Do your harrying early in the morning or in the evening, for then in the natural course of things the female is more ready to leave the nest, and she requires less beckoning from the cock.

In any case if you chase the cock and he fails to help by calling his mate, he will narrow down the area for your search. Whilst being harried, you will find him very attached to one piece of ground. He will fly from one perch to another, and these you will find enclose a definite tract of ground. On the wing he will hover and dip over this same ground, and you may be sure that in it lies his nest. His very song-perches—and the woodlark will sing perched as well as in flight—are often very close to the nest.

Woodlarks are a model of married companionship. It is said that in districts where the species is tolerably common it forms small flocks during the winter. But on ground where there are only scattered birds, the several pairs seem to keep together during the winter months. One pair in particular near my home in North Dorset I regularly see when pheasant shooting in November and December, and in April they nest within a few hundred yards of the winter haunt.

Certainly in the breeding season they are very attached husbands and wives, not only during the courtship phase when such behaviour is to be expected, but also after the eggs are laid and even hatched. During incubation the cock is rarely far away from the hen, and from the moment she leaves her eggs in order to feed, he is her constant companion and guardian. He has a charming way of entertaining her during these meal times by singing in low sub-song and quivering his wings in joy. With the chicks he is as hard-working as his mate. Indeed, woodlarks appear to carry out their domestic duties as very close partners. If it is only on very rare occasions that both birds arrive actually at the nest together, they assuredly go to collect food and return with it together, leaving and arriving in company. One bird will feed, retire and wait for its partner, then off they will go together for more. The next you will know of them will be that quiet, wondrous silvery little *too-lü-ee* as they return. They are utterly charming and quite delightful birds.

If you are lucky, you may hear your woodlark singing by night. I have never been so fortunate, but nocturnal song is a well-known, if irregular, habit. Should you venture on to the heath, however, when the light fails, you will be rewarded, even if the woodlark fails to oblige. For the heath has both a night and day bird-life. Owls it shares with the woods and pastures. The ubiquitous little owl, that pushful alien, has made for itself a niche amongst the fir trees and heather with that same adaptability that in so short a time has led to its spread into breeding grounds so different as a shearwater-frequented islet off the Welsh coast and rabbit warrens on the downland. Tawnies hoot mournfully to each other in mellow responsions. Even a few long-eared owls, now in the south grown so local, almost rare, find like the kestrels convenient nesting sites in the numerous untenanted crows' nests in the pine clumps.

But the true voices of the night on the Dorset heath are the nightjar and the nightingale, the one as eerie and as unmusical as the other is appealing and lovely.

Of the nightjar it is not easy to write. It is a bird of impressions rather than of substance, a voice rather than flesh and blood, a ghost, more a big moth than a bird. Of all night birds it is the most nocturnal, notwithstanding even the owls. Them by day we often flush, or have our attention drawn to them by a host of scolding lesser fry. The nightingale sings more in the hours of daylight than of darkness. Shearwaters, night birds that they are at their breeding stations, we may see by day winging their gliding, effortless way over the waves. But how little does the nightjar appear between dawn and sunset! How rarely indeed is it even flushed! For so long as the sun casts its light over the horizon the nightjar sleeps, and the wonderful camouflage of its immobile, dormant body shields it from all but the most observant eyes.

But as the sun sinks below the western sky, the heath wakes to a new and unexpected life. The great bird chorus is over. A nightingale perhaps intermittently enriches the growing silence with its passionate outburst. The owls, whose noisiest period is just before sunset, call only occasionally, now too busy at their hunting. Everywhere, it seems, life is taking its rest, and the blind seems drawn on activity until dawn again rouses its children. Then from the bracken slope beneath the pine clump there steals on the ear an eerie reeling, louder, more insistent than the self-effacing, vaguely similar 'song' with which the grasshopper warbler in the swampy valley half an hour ago sang the day to rest. This is no quiet lullaby: it is a salute to wakening life.

Listen—you will not be able to help it, unless your ears are deaf to the things around you. The eerie song planes up and down the scale, now loud, now soft, now near, now far, like a motor cycle in the distance. Suddenly it stops. The heath seems very dead and silent without it. Then a sharp *co-ick* smacks into the silence and upsets your ideas that after all it was but a belated salute to night. A crisp crack of wings hitting together brings you up with a start. A strange shape is flitting, hovering, gliding overhead in the growing darkness. Is it real, or a mere figment of the mind that as always in the dusk sees trees move and bushes take on weird shapes? But the ghostly creature calls *co-ick* again, cracks its wings and vanishes, reappearing from another quarter, as though you were a candle to a moth, a thing it cannot leave. Or would it perhaps intimidate you, make you depart to places less haunted than this, its chosen home?

Yet bird it is—though it would seem that earlier generations have not always made that discovery. For in folk lore the nightjar is a thing of evil omen, a doer of dark deeds. Even when they knew it as a bird, did they not call it *Caprimulgus*, the goat-sucker, a witch, turned bird, that sucked the udders of the goats and made barren the cattle? Poor nightjar! For if ever a bird were harmless, it is *Caprimulgus europaeus*, whose most daring deed is the killing of moths! But who are we to blame an age more superstitious than ours for thus regarding so suspicious a creature of such behaviour? In days when the unaccountable was ever explained by witchcraft and before the firearm could kill to prove flesh and blood, it would only be remarkable if the nightjar had escaped obloquy; for if ever a bird asked for suspicion it is this.

The light of day does nothing to dissipate this eerie atmosphere. For if you see the evejar while the sun is up, he will still be 'lone on the fir branch . . . brooding o'er the gloom', a thing seemingly as dead as the old wood his plumage pattern so remarkably resembles. The large eyes which he shares with all creatures of the night will be shut into the thinnest of slits, and his immobile body will move as little as a stuffed specimen in a museum.

The eye shut to a mere slit is, however, deceptive, for it does not indicate that the bird is enjoying a siesta. Before you ever see the nightjar by day, you may rest assured that it has seen you first. And this practice of shutting the eye forms part of the bird's tactics to escape notice. Whilst photographing a pair of nightjars, I watched and portrayed the various positions and phases of this behaviour. On first alighting on an old stump near the nest the eye was always wide open. If nothing disturbed the bird, it remained thus until she was finally incubating the eggs. Then it was half closed as the sitter dozed off. But if I arranged, as on occasions I did by means of silent signals, for the appearance of a human being after the bird had alit, it was a very different story, for the bird's immediate reaction was to lower itself by crouching on its perch, the eye at the same time closing. The nearer the danger got, the lower the bird and the tighter the eye was shut, until in the last stage it lay flattened along the branch, and so little eye was showing that it was remarkable that it could see anything at all. In this position the camouflage of the plumage was quite amazing.

Even so it is assuredly on the ground that the nightjar's protective coloration is seen to best advantage. When the bird is incubating, the eye does not seem to look at it but through it. No British bird, not even the much-quoted woodcock, proves so clearly the powers of disruptive patterning. In the nightjar it is quite remarkable. I have seen even people whose eyes were not unaccustomed to the things of nature stand within a mere three feet of the bird—and it is not a small one—and pick it out only after concentration and effort. In nightjar nest-hunting I have long since ceased to try to find the eggs with my eyes. I merely walk quickly over the ground, quartering it until a previously unnoticed brown form rises from my feet and exposes two white eggs. For a moment it is as though the very broken twigs and dead bracken had come to life and taken flight.

The nightingale is only nocturnal by happy accident. It is in point of fact as much a bird of the day as its near relatives, the robin and the redstart. But nature, with one of her great flashes of genius, has ordained that the finest of all bird songsters shall sing in the hours of stillness. Not a few have tried to assail the nightingale's position as the greatest of our song birds. Thrush, blackbird, lark, wood wren, all are quoted as worthy rivals, as peers or even as better. For myself, although in Provence I have listened to nightingales in such numbers that only the overpowering volume of their sound prevented one from ignoring them, this bird's song is beyond all description worthy of the place it has won in poetry, romance and fable. Nor does it owe its supremacy to the fact that at its greatest hour it has the stage to itself. By day it is still peerless, conspicuous far above all others. But it should be heard at night; for the finest *prima donna* is never at her best in a carol singing party.

I cannot analyse that song. I have listened to it and watched the performer within touching distance of my hide, listened to its vehement appeal, watched the quivering, vibrating body of the bird. But I cannot analyse it. It belongs to that class of beautiful things which defy cold print and the definition of words. You can but listen, and having listened to your fill, remember. Like a glorious sunset the nightingale's song lingers as a memory, in an indefinite way clear in the store-cupboard of the mind, yet impossible to express in words. Is it not the same with all

PLATE 55. *Sparrow Hawk with full-grown chicks*

PLATE 57. *Sparrow Hawk watching her 6-day-old family*

PLATE 56. *Sparrow Hawk with chicks aged 3 days*

beautiful things? For beauty is so subtle a mistress that always she keeps half her cards concealed, lest man should try to make tangible that which is intangible, and destroy it with his vandalism.

Yet certain features of the song permit analysis. To me the opening bars, the rich *lü-lü* notes appeal most. They have an air of expectancy about them which promises much to come. Then the pause, the silence. How well-timed it is! As the rich notes steal forth, you are agog for the main performance. But you must wait. That moment of suspense is most effective, and then follows the spate of passionate song, broken and divided by pauses into many movements. It is the juxtaposition of harshness and of softness, of the loud and of the quiet, of shy appeal and of brazen challenge, which is so brilliant and so subtle. For the song is disjointed. Rich, mellow phrases steal out of the thicket; it seems that the rest must continue in that vein. But harshness surprisingly follows. Yet the song, despite its many breaks and pauses, is an integral whole. Its greatness lies in its contrasts and its pauses, its surprises and its vehemence. Above all this last. The nightingale seems to sing, because if it did not, it would burst. Not only are the notes powerful and far-carrying, but every fibre of its body vibrates to the emotion which produces them. The very feathers of the swollen throat grow rigid and tremble with passion. Of other birds only the wren, blowing its little self up like a balloon and gradually deflating until the song is finished, puts like energy into its singing.

Nightingale song does not cease, as seems popularly supposed, with the hatching of the eggs. I have recorded full song on the tenth day after hatching when the young were large, and my cock bird not infrequently paused to give tongue on his favourite perch on the way to the nest with a beakful of grubs. Yet quite apart from the real song nightingales possess a varied vocabulary used for alarm or 'conversational' purposes. The normal scolding note is a deep, throaty *tuck-tuck* used by a bird anxious at human proximity to its nest. Nearing the nest both birds use a thin *tsweep* call-note to the young, so like the willow wren's alarm call that at first I thought a pair of those leaf warblers must have a nest very close to my hide. It proved however to be only the parent nightingale warning the chicks of its coming. When a cock and hen meet near the nest when busy at their duty, they carry on a loud conversation in harsh grating notes, very far removed from the rich, mellow phrases of the full song.

Behaviour at the nest follows the same general trend as that of its nearest relatives. Feeding falls upon both sexes. In the early stages, when the female is brooding, the main weight of this duty rests upon the shoulders of the cock who hands over the food to the brooding hen for distribution to the young beneath her. When the chicks are of such an age that they can be left, both birds undertake the provision of food, and this they share equally at the rate of about five or six feeds an hour. For certain indefinite periods I noted that the cock fed exclusively: at others the female: often both at similar intervals.

Nest-sanitation plays a noticeable part in their role of behaviour with chicks. On all the many occasions on which I saw it practised and at all ages of the chicks, the faeces were devoured at the nest—except once when the bird flew off with the pellicle in the bill. Every feed in fact ended with the removal of excreta by the parents. The pellicles were indeed deliberately waited for, and if the process of feeding did not automatically produce them, the young were stimulated by prodding.

CHAPTER 5

Southern Woodland

If the birds of northern moor and loch or of European lagoon and sierra have often enticed me far from my own fields and hedgerows, the abundant bird life of southern woods has never lost one iota of its appeal. Indeed whereas the expedition further afield has been merely an isolated incident, the woods and copses around my home have been my daily bread. Returning from the north where birds are thin on the ground, I have rejoiced in their abundance; returning from the south, I have been happy again to see so many familiar friends, to hear again so many well-loved songs. For where can the sheer joy and pleasure of birds be realized to better advantage than in a wood of Southern England in the middle of May? Willow wren and chiffchaff, blackcap and nightingale are amongst the songsters; tits, tree creepers and nuthatches perform acrobatic feats in the trees; green and greater spotted woodpeckers call and drum; and over all the sparrow hawk by day, tawny and little owls by night, hold sway.

Such woodland is the cradle of the ornithologist. It is in it and from it that are gleaned those first-fruits of knowledge and experience from which a more extended appreciation of birds eventually comes. It is meet and right that their birds should hold an especial place in his esteem.

There lies within sight of my house, not two miles away, one such wood on a high ridge of ground. A mixture of oak and conifer, of thick tangled undergrowth and open clearing, it is typical of its kind. If its nature as a pheasant preserve has kept in check the jays and sparrow hawks, its small bird life has benefited in turn. It is rich in warblers. Willow wrens and chiffchaffs share the tangled undergrowth with whitethroats,

63

garden warblers and blackcaps. The wood wren also, in far lesser numbers, honours a few favoured spots to which it is markedly faithful every year. Lesser whitethroats 'rattle' along the confining hedges, and in some years even the grasshopper warbler will reel from a clearing. Tree creepers find many suitable nesting sites, and nuthatches plaster with mud natural holes in the trees. Artificial ones are bored by two species of woodpecker, and all the normal tits, except the willow tit, find sanctuary and a breeding habitat. Goldcrests and spotted flycatchers frequent the keeper's house along with the usual birds of a country garden, thrushes, blackbirds, robins, dunnocks and chaffinches. At dusk the nightjar churs and the nightingale sings while tawny and little owls go about their business.

It cannot claim a single species which calls for special remark, not even the hawfinch or redstart, but it is a perfect wild aviary of those birds which are essentially English, and without which our summer and our countryside would mean much less than they do. It is a wood that can be repeated many times again in nearly every Southern English shire.

Of its small birds the wood wren is my first love. Its song I number amongst the great bird songs, though others would not rate it so high. In all its ways and in its appearance it is a delight. It is to the wood what the grey wagtail is to the stream—the very spirit of the place. No matter on what I am engaged I will always stop to listen to the wood wren, and there is no bird music which my ears register more quickly. In Norfolk, where it is a very local bird indeed, I found a new locality for the wood wren in just this way, for I was neither thinking nor talking of birds, but deeply engaged in a serious conversation, when I heard in a neighbouring wood that refreshing little trill bubble forth. The next day I found its nest. This was the first I have ever seen in a coniferous habitat. The dome of the nest was in fact built of fallen fir needles instead of the normal grass bents, and was consequently even more remarkably concealed than usual.

The normal habitat of the wood wren is however beech or oak wood, usually with a much thinner undergrowth of brambles and bracken than suits the tastes of its two close relatives, the chiffchaff and willow wren. It is also more truly a woodland bird than either of the other two. Willow wrens are usually most plentiful on the edge of a wood; they like also small copses; they do not ignore a rough common with scattered trees, even the ditches beside a road. The chiffchaff has much the

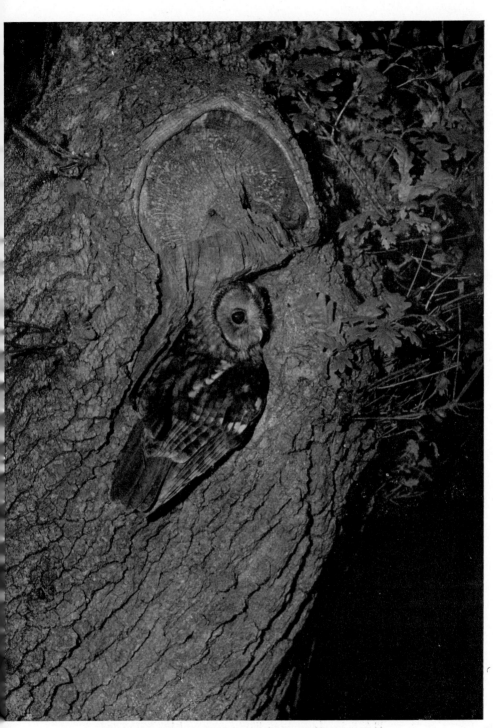

PLATE 58. *Tawny Owl (by flashlight)*

PLATE 59. *Little Owl with earthworm (by flashlight)*

PLATE 60. *Little Owl at entrance to nest*

PLATE 61. *Little Owl staring at hide*

PLATE 67. *Cirl Buntings: pair at nest*

PLATE 68. *Female Cirl Bunting at nest*

same tastes, but it demands the semblance of a wood more than the other. But the wood wren likes a proper wood, and does not necessarily favour its outer fringes. Yet it is often difficult in one wood in which all three of these leaf warblers are nesting to analyse what advantages certain spots, annually occupied by wood wrens, have to offer over many others, apparently alike but ignored by them, and often adopted by willow warblers and chiffchaffs. Why too in three such closely allied species should the last two use feathers for the lining of their nests while the wood wren wholly dispenses with them?

My next love is the nuthatch, a gymnast of a high order, for can he not outdo as a climber all other birds in being able to descend a tree head first? I love his clear call and his delicate colouring, and that nesting hole, plastered with mud until it is of appropriate size, intrigues me, making me wonder how the habit has arisen. Did the nuthatch once bore a hole like the woodpeckers, or did it once nest in a bank like a sand martin? And has it in the course of time evolved this present form of nest as a compromise?

The tree creeper has by contrast no such elaborate ideas. Content with a cleft made by the separation of the bark from the trunk, it makes a simple nest. Simple and elementary too are its movements as a climber, for it runs like a little brown mouse up the trunk, and I have never seen it perform any gymnastic feats, except that of squeezing itself in and out of its nest. But the industry of the bird is phenomenal and invites my heartiest admiration. It always appears so serious and so busy that its life seems to be one round of harassing problems. Yet the tree creeper is not without initiative. It was once one of the birds of the ancient pine forests, like the crested tit. But unlike that last species, as the forests declined, it did not also decline and decrease, but adapted itself to deciduous woodland, where to-day it has made a firm niche for itself. Nor has it been long in learning about the softness of the wood of the comparatively recently introduced Wellingtonia, in a cavity of the bark of which it will find a comfortable roosting-place.

The woodpeckers, famous tree climbers though they are, are also primitive in their methods, lacking the agility and versatility of the nuthatch. Yet the green pecker's laughing cry and the greater spot's drumming and loud alarm note are characteristic sounds of the wood. Of the two the last is the more truly woodland species, and I have never found its nest except where the trees grow thickly. The yaffle on the

E

other hand divides its time between thick cover and open hedgerows surrounding the wood, and I have seen as many nests, if not more, in isolated trees as in true woodland. It is also less arboreal. Green woodpeckers find most of their food on the ground and can often be seen hunting for ants and other insects in fields of short grass, even on a tennis lawn. The greater spot is a true bird of the tree tops, and, were it not for its drumming and alarm call, would be frequently overlooked. Its striking and conspicuous plumage pattern has doubtless dictated this habitat preference.

Not that the yaffle's colour scheme is dull. Indeed with its red head and bright yellow-greens it is at close quarters a very beautiful bird, at the same time wearing a very foolish expression. Its white eyelid and black moustachial streak give it a brainless appearance which closer acquaintance does nothing to remove. It is a clown second only to the puffin. Nor is this impression dispelled by its jerky climbing movements which are most laboured and artificial.

It is however in its rivalry with the starling that the true measure of its intelligence is seen. That a bird of such size and so well equipped with a powerful beak can be so easily and so regularly evicted from its self-made nesting holes must occasion surprise. I was once fortunate enough to watch such an eviction. A yaffle had bored a nesting hole high up in an oak and on this a pair of starlings had their eye. The pecker was in the hole, popping its head in and out in its consternation and indecision at the chattering presence of its tormentors. These were deployed for the attack, one on a branch above the nest, and the other below, and they kept up a continuous stream of vocal abuse. The pecker at last emerged instead of defending its castle from within. One of the starlings nipped into the hole in a trice, while the other scolded and mobbed the rightful owner. When the second woodpecker arrived, it tried to get into the hole. It was a most pitiful sight. It clung to the entrance and popped its head in and out for several minutes, wearing a look of pained surprise at the unfamiliar tenant within. I never saw the starling inside rush to the entrance to frighten away the pecker. It stayed put, clearly believing that possession was nine-tenths of the law. The second starling now harried the second woodpecker and chased it away from the nest. It then stood on guard, and broke up in infancy any attempt at counter-attack by the two yaffles which were climbing disconsolately about the tree. After an hour they flew off, and I doubt not they never returned, for the starlings were in undisputed possession when next I passed the tree.

The greater spotted woodpecker suffers from no such competition. It seems to be in every way a more successful and more adaptable bird, for it is at home in coniferous forests as well as deciduous woodland. It is at present expanding its range, and I remember hearing the food cry of the chicks and finding the nest of a pair in a wood that was just inside the southern boundary of Sutherland. Since then, when out deer-stalking, I have seen its old nesting holes in little patches of birch scrub miles out on the moors of a northern Ross-shire 'forest'. The keeper knew the bird well.

Perhaps my most vivid memory of the greater spot is a misty September day in Shetland when in the gloom I became aware that overnight there had arrived a small invasion of what must clearly have been Scandinavian migrants. In treeless Shetland they had to make do with fence posts instead of their native birches. One bird was so perplexed by the unusual terrain that it committed suicide down the kitchen chimney of the hotel!

Upon this wealth of small bird life prey jays, sparrow hawks and owls which in turn are kept reduced by the keeper's gun. The jay is a thief, the sparrow hawk an assassin; the tawny owl is a murderer by night and the little owl a gangster. At the same time it is to be doubted if the abundance of song birds is really appreciably greater for the accidental protection which game-preservation affords. I know many woodlands which are untended by keepers—and they are becoming ever-increasingly common—where the population of warblers, tits, thrushes and others is no less numerous than in woods where the pheasant is sacrosanct and 'vermin' are ruthlessly destroyed. Nature's 'balance' works by natural laws, and man should not interfere. It gives me little pleasure to see, as I have seen, a little owl incubating amongst a rotting pile of thrushes and starlings; or to watch a sparrow hawk streak through the oaks, make two quick grabs with its feet and in its talons carry off a right and left out of a brood of blue tits just out of the nest. But these things are ordained as part of the natural scheme. The keeper's gibbet of 'vermin' has no such authority: it is the creation of man sitting in a seat of judgment for which he is not fitted, save that he invented the trap and the gun. It is a sight of horror.

The nocturnal habits of the owls keep them partly out of the way.

Bird Haunts in Southern England

The jay and sparrow hawk have achieved self-effacement by cunning. For a bird that is undoubtedly common how often do we see a jay to good advantage? To me it is more a harsh voice in the undergrowth of saplings than a bird of flesh and blood. Stray glimpses of its conspicuous plumage it affords only as it sneaks off—a crafty bird like all the tribe of the crows to which it belongs. But I cannot approve of its thieving and murderous tactics, egg-sucking and chick-snatching.

The sparrow hawk by contrast is a clean killer, which admittedly takes a heavy toll of small bird-life. Identification from a hide of prey brought to the chicks in the nest is never easy, for it is often decapitated or at least roughly plucked before it arrives. In the one nest at which I watched he development of the young from hatching to flying it was small birdstwhich predominated, particularly tits. That this hawk should incur the gamekeeper's enmity is perhaps natural, yet a study of its methods of hunting suggests that the hatred it has won for itself has been exaggerated.

The sparrow hawk is a killer in true chase. It takes its prey flying, either by straight pursuit, twisting over a hedge into a flock of starlings, or by a snatch and grab raid in the tree tops. I have never seen a sparrow hawk pounce to earth; it kills on the wing.[1] Hence feather rather than fur figures very largely in its diet sheet. So far as the toll it takes of game is concerned, this hunting technique must be borne in mind. It will be granted that an adult pheasant is beyond its powers: a full-grown partridge is just a possible victim, especially for the female, and indeed has been recorded. As it sweeps suddenly over a hedge, it must often panic a feeding covey into flight—a tempting target, but one calling for a tremendous output of strength to tackle. The adult game bird can be ruled out as anything but exceptional prey.

The chicks, however, are well within its powers, but here its non-pouncing habit has an important bearing, for young partridges or pheasants in their early stages crouch on the approach of danger. There follows, however, a period in their development when they tend to flush and fly weakly when alarmed or disturbed, as they would be with a sparrow hawk streaking down a woodland ride or glade. These few weeks in June are the danger point, and it is then, and then only, that

[1] A sparrow hawk will of course come to the ground to retrieve a kill which has fallen to earth or at which it has been disturbed when plucking it. Thus are they trapped. But the kill itself is normally made in flight.

PLATE 69. *Cirl Buntings tending chicks*

PLATE 70. *Lesser Spotted Woodpecker, male with beakful of aphides*

this hawk is a real potential menace. Even so, it must be remembered that this is also the month of the year when other prey, small birds and their broods, is most plentiful. If a sparrow hawk kills one pheasant chick, he will kill for it infinitely more tits, starlings or warblers.

For a species against which the hand of man is so ruthlessly turned the sparrow hawk is a bird of outstanding courage. This is only revealed in the defence of its nest and chicks, for at other times it adopts the tactics of the other avian Ichabods, jays and carrion crows, of avoiding man at all costs. Only rarely will you see a sparrow hawk in a wood. It will be gone at the very first sign of approaching danger, turning and twisting through the trees, keeping the timber between you and itself. From its nest too it will slip away quickly and quietly in the hope of being over-looked. But build a hide and a very different character emerges. I have worked three pairs of sparrow hawks from hides, and all three have been brave to the point of folly. All so rapidly became accustomed to interfer-ence that kicking the nesting tree, even in one case throwing sticks at her from the hide, failed to move the brooding bird.

The female of my last pair was the best example. When the hide was only just begun, she would return to her nest in my fully exposed pres-ence twelve feet away and glare and scream defiance at me. In the later stages of the operation, whenever I put my face through the sacking, she would dash into the attack, flicking the hide roof with her wings (or feet) as she flashed by—a picture of indignant rage. And can any bird look so angry? That piercing yellow eye is the wildest thing in nature.

There is however another side. When her fears are allayed and she is undisturbed, looking after her chicks, the rage and cruelty in her eye mellow, and she plays and looks the part of fond mother as ably as any warbler. As with most birds of prey, the nest is essentially the female's sphere of influence, the male being mainly responsible for the provision of food. Normally he will call the hen off the chicks to take the prey, but in the later stages, when she is not in constant attendance at the nest, if she does not respond to his call, he will come down himself, deposit the kill and is away. But his visits are very fleeting, and he does not stop to administer the food to the young.

For the first week after the hatching of the eggs the female spends the day with them, alternately brooding and feeding. At about that time she ceases continual brooding, but stands by them watching, as it were, over their well-being. On the sixteenth day she begins to leave them for ever-increasing periods, but is quick to return if heavy rain or a chill wind should come on. Thereafter she gives them more and more independence. I noticed the first attempts at 'branching', climbing out of the nest, on the twenty-second day. On the same day food was not torn up and apportioned by the female, but deposited and left for the chicks to carve. The young at this stage were growing very restless. By the twenty-fifth day all are 'branching' to some considerable distance from the nest, which they appear to use only as a dining table and presumably at night. A dining table indeed it continues to be even when they are on the wing for at least another fortnight. Wing-flapping is characteristic of this period, even short 'flights' across the nest, and there is an atmosphere of general restlessness, much preening of the last of the down feathers and leg-stretching and talon-clenching.

The two common woodland owls of the south, tawny and little, do not afford the same opportunities for observation. Nocturnal for the greater part, they hide away their lives in the darkness, and their presence is known chiefly from their calls.

Until recently even the sparrow hawk has not called upon itself greater hatred from the game-preserver and bird-watcher than the little owl. It had not a friend in the world. It was always the fiend incarnate, the blood-lustful killer of game chicks and young birds. While no one would deny that it does damage, the inquiry into its food conducted by the British Trust for Ornithology revealed that there is another side to the picture. Although small birds and mammals form a big portion of its diet, yet insects predominate. Undoubtedly the food varies with individuals. I have found a little owl sitting in its nest hole amid a regular feather bed of dead starlings and small birds, but most nests on examination are littered not with feathers but with insect remains.[1] The use of flash by bird photographers has more than confirmed that insects form a vast proportion of the food of the chicks. In the two pairs I have myself worked no fur or feather came to my notice. I hold no brief for the little owl. For me it is still, and will always be, a species we have obtained by artificial means, and therefore undesirable, but I do not believe it to be half the sinner it has been painted by so many.

Nevertheless we could have done without the little owl. Before its

[1] It should be noted that in the case of the nest containing birds incubation had only just begun. I am inclined to think that their presence is to be accounted for as 'courtship offerings' rather than as food for the larder.

general introduction it had occurred in this country, so that it may perhaps legitimately have a place on the British list. Its present status however must be attributed wholly to human agency, for since the first introductions into Kent and Northamptonshire in the 'eighties and 'nineties of last century, this alien has forged ahead in such a remarkable manner that to-day it has spread into most parts of England and Wales up to the Borders, and in some districts it is a really abundant bird. While a natural niche must have been ready for it here, it is doubtful if we shall ever know the ecological cause of its success. One factor in its favour however is obvious. Not even the pushful starling can outdo it in adaptability. It can find a suitable nesting site not only in the woodland trees, but in buildings and outhouses, better suited to the barn owl. A rabbit-hole in a downland warren will not deter it, nor even a small hole amongst the rocks of a Welsh island, where incidentally it played havoc with the Manx shearwaters.

Naturally such a phenomenal success has raised the whole question of the justification of such introductions. Opinions differ about the artificial increase or decrease of alien forms of life, but to any thinking naturalist such methods *must* be regarded as most undesirable. To him who makes the original move the whole scheme may appear as an interesting experiment without much hope of success. That attitude is incorrect. For if success should occur, the results cannot be foreseen. Australia and New Zealand come readily to mind as two countries which have learnt their lesson with both animal and vegetable introductions. Indeed, even the re-introduction of lost species must be viewed with suspicion, and although we may be glad to see, for instance, the capercaillzie back in our northern forests, yet it would be a mistake to conclude from that harmless success that it would necessarily be desirable to have restored artificially all our lost birds.

The little owl, however, is here and is now a common British bird. If we are rightly reluctant hosts, yet it must be admitted that it is not without some fascination. I well remember seeing a pair perched side by side on a telegraph pole in Andalucia, looking so delightful that for a moment I could readily understand the motives which influenced the original introducers to bring it across to English woods and fields. Its attractive habit of bobbing at the knees, its big yellow staring eyes are not without their charm. One bird I photographed in the cavity of an oak tree kept me continually amused whenever it ran down the long hollow of its home. I used to amuse myself, and check the bird, by clicking my tongue when it got half-way. Out went its feet and all brakes were applied, while it glared in indignation at the hide. When it retired within to sit, I would click again, and out it would run to the entrance, glare at the hide, almost shrug its shoulders and go back inside. It was difficult to resist doing this continuously, for the expression was exactly that of a hard-worked housewife who had been disturbed by small boys ringing the front-door bell and running away.

The little owl is generally credited with being slightly more diurnal than the other species, except the short-eared. While it is certainly on the move during daylight hours more often than the long-eared or tawny owls, it is in my experience mainly nocturnal. It is seen more often by day because it roosts in places more subject to disturbance. Certainly at the nest, except for the period of incubation and immediately after hatching, when incidentally all the owls become temporarily diurnal, I have *never* known it feed its chicks by day. For the first seven days the chicks are brooded, and if the owl was disturbed, she would return while the sun was yet up. Thereafter they were wholly neglected during the daytime, and consistent feeding of them did not begin till about 9.15 p.m. (B.S.T.) on a June evening.

The tawny owl is similar in its nesting biology. The first pair I worked had built in an open tree-nest of indeterminable origin. It was so decrepit in fact that I built most of it myself! The parent owl brooded the one youngster (until he fell out!) for a week. After that she was never seen in the daytime. Indeed the tawny loathes daylight and is reluctant even to be flushed.

I worked a second pair in May 1940, and here feeding did not begin until it was too dark to see the bird at the nest-hole, about three-quarters of an hour later than the little owls. If she perched first on a side branch of the parent tree, I could just distinguish her as a silhouette, but for her arrival at the nest I had to rely only on the sound of the scrape of her talons as she alit—a most ghostly bird.

This second nest caused me a little embarrassment. It was sited near a wood, close to a country lane. I had to build a pylon hide which was conspicuous. As I was using flash, the hide was further decorated with a staring reflector. It was the time of the invasion of Holland and the paratroop scare was on. Once I had the number of my car taken. But this was nothing to one evening when I suddenly found myself being stalked by a patrol of Scotsmen. I shall never forget the corporal's face when I put my head out to explain. I was wearing a fencing mask (the tawny, if it attacks, is our only really dangerous bird). It was greatly to his northern credit that he understood the mad doings of a bird photographer, and I would not have blamed him if he had put me in the guard room—or the local asylum!

CHAPTER 6

Orchard and Pasture in Somerset

Not for nothing is Somerset famous for its cider. The apples which produce it grow profusely throughout the county in a forest of orchards. These may be extensive and as well tended as an ornamental show garden, or they may be small extensions of what is really only a little vegetable plot, often little cultivated and allowed to grow and mature in their own sweet way, undisciplined and with perhaps only a very occasional visit from the owner until the fruit crop is ripe for the picking. Save at this harvest time they remain undisturbed for the rest of the year.

These apple orchards form little oases of bird life in the surrounding pastoral countryside of hedges and cultivated fields. They cannot claim a characteristic avifauna of their own, for they do not seem to attract any one species as their unique denizen. They are, however, in themselves noticeably beloved of birds for nesting purposes, and, tending as they do to form concentration areas, afford within comparatively small confines an excellent habitat for many different species, all of which are most probably present in the surrounding hedges and woods, but far more scattered over the ground. For that reason you will be wise to let the orchard attract you with your field glasses, especially the small wild orchard where the trees, receiving no careful attention, are the victims of aphis, and where disease has rotted the branches and left gaping holes. Such a place is a living museum of the bird life of many acres of its surroundings, clearly a most desirable habitat, where doubtless only the most favoured—or strongest—have carved a territory.

For within its narrow boundaries there will be a pair or two of one and all the species found in the surrounding hedgerows and woods. Chaffinches will build their lichen-covered nests in the forks of the apple trees or in its hedges just as they do in the hawthorns by the lane and surrounding the farmer's open fields. Yellow hammers will spend the long summer day wheezing out their dry notes with the same monotony that can be heard along the roadside near by. Song thrushes and blackbirds will hardly be more or less common here than they are in the next field, garden or spinney. And there will be sparrows, robins and dunnocks in normal numbers. In short the orchard, unlike the pond or the heath, does not attract a typical bird population of its own. Yet it is well worthy to be classed as a specific bird haunt by virtue of its obvious attraction for birds.

Four species, however, I would call primarily orchard birds—the mistle thrush, goldfinch, wryneck and lesser spotted woodpecker. There is not one of these which you will not find breeding in other types of country, but all are such obvious dwellers in the orchard that such a haunt must be regarded as their first choice. The mistle thrush's place may be questioned, for it will nest quite literally wherever there are trees. An old yew in the garden, a young elm in the wood, a laurel in the park, a pine in a moorland copse, even, as I write, a plane tree round a barrack square, all alike are welcome to this bird. But orchards he loves beyond all else, and while you may hunt park, garden or copse without finding a resident pair, you will find few orchards that do not provide nesting cover for at least one family of mistle thrushes. Here on the leafless apple trees the cock will challenge January's cold and February's rain with that defiant song, and later his nest will be built on the naked tree as though he wished the whole world to know his secret, and often before the blossom is off, the young will be out of the nest.

When the mistle thrush first has eggs in the nest, the goldfinches are still around the rough commons and waste ground from which since autumn they have won a livelihood of seeds, but these winter flocks are rapidly breaking up, and there is a marked movement towards the hedgerows and gardens where, when the leaf is on the trees, they will nest and spend the summer. Of these the orchard will take as many pairs as the unwritten laws of territory and distribution will allow, for if there is any bird which loves the fruit tree, it is the goldfinch. Here in Somerset—and where better, for has not Hudson for all time coupled the goldfinch with Ryme Intrinsica?—in the orchards and gardens and along the roadside hedges these delightful little birds now abound.

It is difficult for those of my generation to believe that not very long ago the goldfinch was sufficiently uncommon to be regarded as a bird of note—though to judge by Hudson it was common in this district thirty years ago. Such changes of status in bird populations are a fascinating study, but only a few lend themselves to scientific inquiry. Mr. James Fisher's painstaking report on the fulmar petrel is a case in point. But the small bird of the hedgerow does not allow this type of census and assessment. Why has the goldfinch increased? The bird-catcher no longer—openly at least—spreads his lime to put it in a cage for sale. Waste ground with its thistles—and food is normally behind increases in the animal world—has decreased rather than increased. The fact remains that if the goldfinch was once regarded as comparatively uncommon, to-day it abounds. And may it long continue to do so, for there is no more charming small bird of English gardens and lanes.

With the wryneck the Somerset orchard is hardly concerned, for if the species still breeds there, it has never crossed my path, nor have I even heard that loud clarion call with which it advertises its arrival in the early morning of a mid-April day. It is a bird of the orchards of Kent where I know it best, but where to-day it is decreasing rapidly and at a most alarming rate.

The lesser spotted woodpecker, however, is a characteristic species of the Somerset orchards. Never abundant and often absent from many apparently suitable places, it is nevertheless as easily found amongst the apple trees as anywhere else. At least, in my own experience, I know it outside the orchard country only as an unusual bird, a species which one bumps into unexpectedly—almost in fact a rarity. Every ornithologist has the experience of finding that certain birds, of no particular rarity, seem always to elude him. Such to me has been this little woodpecker. I remember in my Oxford days finding my first nest in an old apple tree near Otmoor. I remember finding another some years later, high up in a very decayed elm in a park. I photographed a pair which were breeding in an old alder tree in a Devon coomb. Yet between these three occasions a score or so of casual glimpses would easily cover the sum total of my acquaintance with this bird. For me it has always proved itself elusive and avoided my path. That I came to know it at all well and to regard it as a comparatively normal bird of my ornithological experience was due to the orchards of Somerset. Here it

PLATE 72. *Lesser Spotted Woodpecker, female approaching nest*

PLATE 71. *Lesser Spotted Woodpecker, female at nest-hole*

PLATE 73. *Corn Bunting*

breeds in fair numbers, and if it is not present in every apparently suitable haunt, no bird watcher can explore these apple trees without meeting with it. And certainly if I were asked to show anyone this species, I would without question take him to the apple orchard.

The first barred woodpecker I photographed had a nest with fresh eggs. Both sexes were constantly at the nest hole. Differentiation between male and female is fortunately easy, for the cock has a fine crimson crown which gives him a patch of colour that lifts him aesthetically far above the female, although the rest of her plumage pattern matches his exactly. It has been stated that the cock takes 'the night shift' of incubation. A friend, inspecting this nest at dawn, certainly reported that it was the cock which emerged when the tree was tapped. Yet in the afternoon he was constantly changing places with his lady in the hole. However as the full clutch, so far as a reflector glass could reveal, had only just been completed, serious incubation may not yet have begun, and as I was unable to see anything more of this pair of birds, I cannot say whether he showed similar interest in the eggs at a later stage.

This first nest was situated about thirty feet up a slender alder in a Devon coomb. Later in the same summer in a small Somerset orchard I worked another barred woodpecker's nest which was the lowest of which I have ever heard. Indeed, unless it were a burrow in the ground itself it could hardly have been lower, for the entrance hole was exactly three feet from the ground. In fact the whole broken old apple stump in which it was constructed was only six feet high. More normal sites galore were present both in the same orchard and in neighbouring ones. What influence is it that makes a bird apparently throw all caution to the winds and depart from the rule of its kind?

The liking which the barred woodpecker has for the orchard is doubtless partially due to the abundance of old timber suitable for excavation of nesting holes, and old apple wood is particularly friable. Food supply is however clearly a big factor in this preference. In the woods and parkland insect life is abundant, but it is nowhere as plentiful as in the apple orchard which is not carefully tended and where the harmful aphis reigns supreme. Even a short experience of these orchard-haunting lesser spotted woodpeckers will show the observer that it is the small untended orchard where the trees may grow without the fruit grower's serious attention that is the most popular breeding locality. In fact, the elaborate apple orchard where the dead wood is carefully removed and the trees treated against aphis is not usually favoured by a pair of these attractive little woodpeckers.

This second pair of birds fed exclusively on aphis, and both the speed at which it was collected and the bulging quantity with which the parents' bills were stuffed bore eloquent testimony to the good work these little birds were doing in that quiet orchard. Both sexes fed, and at very frequent intervals indeed, though the female certainly took upon her shoulders the lion's share of the work. It was, however, noticeable that both male and female worked in shifts. For an hour or so the hen woodpecker would pay visits to the young at intervals which only rarely exceeded five minutes and often indeed were so short that one wondered how she contrived to obtain the insect food so quickly.

Then would come a pause and the feverish activity would die down. The incessant food calls of the chicks, always noisy and always hungry, would grow almost desperate. A baby head would for a flash emerge as though to tell his parents the more clearly of the family's disapproval of the breakdown in the messing arrangements. Then suddenly the male would begin feeding, and with the exception of perhaps one visit for the next hour there would be no sign of the female. After that time, as though by mutual arrangement, she would resume and he would retire from active co-operation. On all my many sessions on this pair this routine was most noticeable. Grey days and rain also slowed up the speed of feeding, while bright sunshine seemed to increase its frequency. Cleaning out the nest, so far as I saw, was done only by the male. After three or four visits with food he would enter the hole and emerge with excreta.

Somerset's fame for cider is only equalled by its dairy-farming. Much of that flat country in the east of the county is given over to pasture. It is a land of fields and hedgerows, with little scenery of note, featureless and rather dull. Nor would it appear to harbour any birds that might not be found in the fields and hedges of many another similar part of Southern England. Yet this peaceful country is the home of one very local species—the cirl bunting, that much-confused, easily overlooked bird which seems more at home on sunny Mediterranean shores than ours.

Here in England it is not easily restricted to any particular habitat. It is one of those birds, confined in range and local status, which defies a neat delineation of its haunts. A species like the bearded tit can be nicely tabulated—'requires large reed beds: confined to the Broads' district of East Anglia'. But not the cirl bunting, nor others like it, for instance the woodlark. You bump into the cirl bunting often when you least expect it. There is no doubt that it is frequently overlooked by those who do not know its song, which is often confused with the rattle of the lesser whitethroat. The casual observer might well pass it by as a yellow hammer, and indeed in the female there is ample justification, for separation calls for closer scrutiny than a free and wild bird will often afford.

The resemblance of the male yellow hammer and the male cirl bunting is however only superficial. Seen, as so often we do see the small birds of the lanes and hedgerows, as a mere flash vanishing into the hawthorns or brambles, the cirl bunting seems a yellow-headed, brown-backed bird, an impression which tallies exactly with our usual hasty view of a yellow hammer. But see him at his singing or at close quarters and he is a very different bird, for the yellow of his head is broken by a dark band through the eye and defined in its extent on his chin by a conspicuous black bib. Is it imagination that the brown streakings of his back are richer? The colour of the rump at least is no imagination. A yellow hammer, male or female, slipping into a bush shows a rich brown rump to the watcher's glasses. Your cirl bunting is olive green in this part of its anatomy. This is a character to note, for it is the only one in the field which will serve to separate the females of the two species.

Good as these plumage distinctions are, at any rate for the male birds, it will be almost certainly song which finds and locates for you this local and rather elusive bunting. The song post is normally a tall hedgerow elm. Cirl buntings like to sing high and in good cover. The yellow hammer is content with a tall hawthorn spray from which to wheeze out his 'cheesy' notes. His more local relative prefers to claim his territory from a higher vantage point, and any curious rattling song issuing from such a tree is worthy of investigation.

The song itself is only vaguely reminiscent of the buntings. It is a rattle and is not at all unlike the lesser whitethroat's full song. Once heard it is not readily forgotten, and once known it will lead you to the discovery of more cirl buntings than ever will your eyes and field glasses. But one word of caution, a singing cirl bunting is not easily seen. The top of a hedgerow elm in full leaf provides ample cover, and the singer knows how to make good use of it.

Habitat is difficult to define. Juniper is a favourite shrub, and the downland haunts of this bird have usually at least a sprinkling of this bush. It is also more of a woodland bird than other buntings, by which must not be implied that it frequents the thick undergrowth of the bigger woods, but that it is not averse to the small copse. But I know the cirl bunting best in the fields and hedges of the orchard lands of Somerset and in the high-hedged lanes of Devon. A typical haunt is a pastoral countryside—grass fields with untidy thick hedges of hawthorn, bramble and briar, and above all with elm trees growing at intervals along them. Even here it is patchily distributed. I know a small area of Somerset where most of my work on this species has been done in which it tends to form little colonies. There are many square miles of this type of country but by no means all is inhabited by cirl buntings. Large tracts of it produce never a bird. Then quite suddenly you hear one cock bird, and then another, then a third and so on.

In winter the cirl bunting forms small flocks. One such I had the good fortune to observe daily in the course of my regular duties in a Dorset barracks. The flock was mixed with the sexes about equal in number, and they fed regularly on the sides of a railway cutting which ran through the camp. They were noticeably sedentary and could always be found within 200 yards of this spot until in April they dispersed to their breeding territories.

Song—at least snatches of it—first began on fine days in March, and was full by mid-April, though never as early as that so incessant as it later became when the mayfly came up on the river in the early days of June. For although a resident species the cirl bunting does not on that account nest early. Eggs can be found in May, but June and July are in my experience more certain seasons to find its untidy typical bunting-like nest, the whereabouts of which are often advertised to the world by long straggling bents of dried grass which lead one through the thick cover of the brambles as paper guides the runners in a paper-chase.

I have never seen the cock bird incubating. This seems to be the task of the hen, but he is responsible for feeding her at intervals in his singing. When the chicks hatch, both birds feed. As with most passerine birds, during the first few days after hatching the female broods the young, and the male seems to be solely responsible for food. As the chicks grow stronger, both birds undertake this task. Both too are particular about nest-sanitation, especially the male. This is a point I have observed in

PLATE 75. *Corn Bunting near nest*

PLATE 74. *Corn Bunting at nest*

PLATE 77. *Yellow Wagtail fanning tail*

PLATE 76. *Yellow Wagtail perched*

PLATE 79. *Whinchat—male*

PLATE 78. *Whinchat—female*

PLATE 81. *Grasshopper Warbler*

PLATE 80. *Male Reed Bunting*

PLATE 82. *Marsh Warbler at nest*

PLATE 83. *Marsh Warbler*

PLATE 85. *Marsh Warbler on osier*

PLATE 84. *Reed Warbler sitting*

PLATE 87. *Sedge Warbler approaching nest*

PLATE 86. *Sedge Warbler at nest*

many species, that the male seems more careful about removing excreta than the female. It may be mere impression, but I think not. It is certainly the case in the jay. The young are often prodded after feeding to encourage the appearance of the faeces, and if the parents are not present at the time, the pellicle is deposited on the rim of the nest for later removal.

CHAPTER 7

Sedgemoor

The wide level of Sedgemoor, which once bogged the army of Monmouth and killed the immediate hopes of the Protestant revolt against the rising tyranny of Stuart Catholicism, to-day lies quiet and peaceful, when viewed from the higher ground near Langport—a realm of dykes and osier beds, of luxuriant marsh growth and deep pasture. Although no modern army would now be stopped by its waterways, the wanderer may find his course frequently barred by unexpected ditches that are hidden behind the lush grass of the cattle pastures. Devious indeed is the path of him who would wander off the main droves, which are the arterial roads of this marshland.

It was a warm evening at the end of May when I first drove down through typical Somerset orchards and parked my car where the rustic lane at last gave up the ghost, and developed into a wide cart-track that led across 'the Moor'. The transition was sudden. Except for the dykes on either side of the road with their pollarded willows, the farm lands and orchards were typical Somerset, yet in a trice they ceased, and the marshland won. Before me lay a land where the only indication of farming was the browsing cattle. Reed cutters were plying their knives and piling their osiers ready for later basket work. Reed buntings took the place of chaffinches, and yellow wagtails of their more domestic pied relations. A corncrake called from the lush grass of a pasture by the drove, and from the ditch-side vegetation came the harsh but pleasing songs and vituperations of sedge warblers. A corn bunting, jingling his creaky apology of a song from a marsh gate-post, and a fine cock whin-chat, proclaiming his alarm from an osier stump, recalled for a moment

82

the drier land that lay behind, but the grasshopper warbler that reeled from the osiers and the mallard that rose from the ditch proved, if any proof were wanting, that the character of the bird life had changed as abruptly as that of the country itself.

Sedgemoor holds no famous place in ornithological geography. It is no Hickling Broad or Hermaness. Yet if the one of these two famous bird reserves is associated with the bearded tit and bittern, and the other with the great skua, it is giving away no secret to say that Sedgemoor might claim equal fame as *the* stronghold of the marsh warbler. For this level, devoted to the pasturing of cattle and the industry of reed-cutting, holds within its osier beds probably a greater and more concentrated breeding population of this rare and local warbler than any other specific part of England. The Severn Valley and Upper Thames may hold in sum total a greater number of breeding pairs, but there the ornithologist must search through scattered localities to find this species. Sedgemoor, on the other hand, is a concentration area—a fact of which the egg-collectors are unfortunately only too well aware.

Thus it was that I headed into 'the Moor' down the old drove road. It was yet early for my quarry, for the marsh warbler is amongst the latest of summer migrants, and for a while I took stock of the ordinary breeding birds. First in abundance clearly came reed-buntings. The black-and-white-headed cock birds wheezed out their sleepy ditties from all corners, and as I crossed one marsh, I flushed five hens from nests, each with from four to five streaked eggs. Another held young chicks, and both cock and hen were feeding at rapid intervals, between most feeds removing the excreta with their bills and flying off with it over the marsh.

Their nesting sites were varied. Some nests were situated on the edge of the osier beds before the vegetation became too thick. Others were in the rough marshes, where reed and rush won the conflict with the attempts of lush grass to oust them. Favourites above all were the stumps of osiers in those beds of recent cutting. The cattle pastures, the delight of the yellow wagtails, were little favoured by reed buntings, which noticeably avoided also the osier beds in full growth, where doubtless views were too restricted and the vegetation too dense.

If the reed bunting characterized the rush and reed marshes, the yellow wagtail was equally *the* species of the open marshes, where the luxuriant grass, growing as it only does where the land is subjected to frequent and healthy flooding, provides fodder in abundance for cattle. Everywhere their sharp little alarm notes called attention to their presence. Often it came from a ball of yellow glory perched upon a gate-post: often too in flight: sometimes from a bird that ran in alarm before me as I walked down the drove. The females, when duly wakened by their mate's anxiety, would join their husbands in their anguish. Yellow wagtails get very alarmed for the safety of their brood, and as with undulating flight, their long tails seeming almost more than they can control, they fly around the intruder's head, it seems that at any moment they will suddenly fall to earth, exhausted by their anguish. Yet often enough they need have no fear, for they know as well as any bird how to conceal their nests, and a bigger danger far than man are the heavy hooves of the lumbering cattle, without which to a yellow wagtail a water meadow is but half the ideal home.

A few pairs of corn buntings share these lush pastures—the ugliest bird in Britain! If any bird is ugly, it must be granted that the corn bunting is an easy winner—stout of beak, indelicate of figure, drab of colour, undoubtedly boorish in manners, and with as little musical ability as a cricket. Aesthetically it is difficult to sing his praises, for he outrages all our finer senses. Yet it is doubtful if a more interesting small bird exists in Britain.

His habits are those of an Arabian sheik, and where corn buntings are common, the harem is the rule rather than the exception, with the male influence as dominant as the female is weak. Watch a cock corn bunting at his singing perch: observe the cock-sureness of his stance, the way he looks all round him (it is not fear), above all the cold glint that comes into his eyes, before with fleshy legs dangling he launches forth to harry another of his kind. Maybe it is another cock that has strayed outside the bounds of his own territory: more likely it is his wife—or one of them— that has had the audacity to feel hungry and to leave her eggs for a brief meal. Ruthlessly she is chivvied back to her job, chased right and left over the field, on to the ground, anywhere, everywhere, until in despair the wretched female drops back on to her nest, so far as I can ever see, unfed and unrefreshed. Indeed, quite when female corn buntings do feed always mystifies me. I like to think of them stealing off by night, when the darkness hides them from their domineering lords.

Certain it is, in my own observations at least, that the cock gives no helping hand. His summer life is that of a gross egotist, a conceited bully

PLATE 88. *Sedgemoor—Osier Beds*

PLATE 89. *Exmoor—Ring Ouzel Valley*

PLATE 90. *Male Stonechat on gorse*

of the first order. Watch him now give tongue from the solitary withy that grows by the dyke side. Completely lost in a sudden onrush of his own importance, he straightens his legs, his fat body draws itself out (if such a little barrel can ever grow slimmer), and his head is thrown back. A cascade of harsh jingling notes is his testimony to his own glory —not once, but twice, thrice or more times, with between each a hasty survey of the neighbourhood, as though he is hurt at the lack of applause. Yet for all his lack of attractiveness he is not unworthy of some admiration. He is lord of a realm and of a harem, and he rules both with a rod of iron.

The polygamous, dictatorial habits of the corn bunting have been fully observed and recorded, but much remains to be done on the distribution of his species; much, too, from that study to be learnt about the influence of soils and vegetation on the status of a bird. For what can account for the patchy way in which the corn bunting is distributed throughout Great Britain—and abroad? In Shetland it is the commonest passerine bird of the little hamlets: it abounds near Land's End: abroad it is widely distributed. Nowhere rare, it yet is absent entirely from many localities between these widely separated regions.

In my own countryside on the borders of Dorset and Somerset it is an unknown bird except on one narrow strip of cultivated ground. Here on a narrow belt of about four miles long and at most a mile wide a number of pairs appear annually. They seem to be as constant and consistent, as though they dwelt within a reserve with wire caging. They have a self-established pale, and I have never seen them outside its well-defined boundaries.

This isolated, insignificant example is worth quoting only because scores of such illustrations of patchy distribution might be collected from many parts of the country. The corn bunting is a common bird and widespread, but why is it abundant in one locality, yet totally absent from another, to all intents and purposes apparently identical in vegetation and soil, and often next door to the favoured area? The bunting family sets many distributional problems, for the same questions arise with the cirl bunting, although its distribution in this country is by no means so extensive.

The whinchat, which here on Sedgemoor shares the cattle pastures with yellow wagtails and corn buntings, is also patchily distributed. Appearing often where it is least expected, it is equally often absent from haunts in which it might well be anticipated. Thus it breeds in the bracken-strewn coombs of Exmoor, but is not found on the apparently equally suitable Dorset heaths. Indeed for this last county there are very few definite breeding records, and the only birds I have seen there have been on passage, here to-day and gone to-morrow. On Sedgemoor it is frequently met with, especially in the cattle pastures. Like the yellow wagtail it finds the bovine association productive of insect food, and both these birds can be seen dancing attendance on their unwitting friends, like miniature cattle egrets.

These four passerines—reed and corn buntings, yellow wagtail and whinchat—cannot fail to invite the attention of the bird-watcher whose steps take him over Sedgemoor's ditches and dykes. Yet as the thicker marsh vegetation is approached and the lush grass gives place to reed and rush and thin swaying osiers form veritable jungles of undergrowth, the bird life changes along with the plants.

From the edge of the osier bed a strange reeling that rises and dies away with surprising speed, most ventriloquial in effect, reveals the hidden presence of a grasshopper warbler. Move quietly: watch carefully, and if you are lucky, you will see the little brown bird at his singing, perched on a withy just clear of the undergrowth, rarely far above, for the grasshopper warbler never lingers far from the thick cover in which it spends its life. Indeed only when he sings will you ever see him, unless it is at the nest, and even then you will probably mistake him for a mouse as he runs through the herbage. Not even the rail family more dislike wide horizons. But when he sings, he often breaks cover and, losing himself utterly in the strange passion of his song, he will at times admit your scrutiny.

The field glasses will reveal a small brown bird, most attractively streaked with darker brown and with a bulbous tail, hard-pressed against his perch and fanned out wide. Watch his head, and as it sways and turns from side to side, you will know the secret of his ventriloquism: you will learn, too, why his song is so pleasing for all its lack of true musical ability, for does not every feather on his throat quiver with the vehemence of his feeling? The corn bunting, fat and ugly, that we found thus lost to all the world in the cattle pastures, only repels our aesthetic senses more when he sings, but the little grasshopper, churring his quavering notes from his withy, is nothing but delightful. Where the one is arrogant, the other is meek.

Sedgemoor

To me the grasshopper warbler is a charming bird, bashful and retiring, and I love the mysterious churring of his music even though, as often as not, he hides his sober identity from my eyes. The rank vegetation which is his haunt becomes in some strange way enriched by his soft mysterious reeling.

Few nests are more difficult to find than his. Most ground-nesting birds have learnt full well the rules of nest concealment, some relying upon the natural camouflage of their eggs like the stone curlew or ring plover, others putting their trust in the deep cover of dense undergrowth. Yet a pair of field glasses will soon disclose the stone curlew's secret, and even the well-hidden nests of whinchat or stonechat will fall victims to the patience of a bird-watcher's telescope, especially if they have chicks. In addition the sitting lark or pipit may be flushed at the feet from their eggs. But none of these methods avail aught with the grasshopper warbler. To watch him you have first to find him, and if you find him, it will be only for a moment before the herbage swallows him up again. Though there are chicks in the nest, it will profit you nothing, for he is no whit less careful in his approach.

Sedge warblers and whitethroats and others of his kind will from time to time make sudden appearances in the open with a beakful of grubs in the vicinity of the nest, but not the grasshopper. With chicks as with eggs, in the breeding season and out of it, he keeps to the depth of the undergrowth. Nor will you flush him, as you may other small birds. Tap the osier stump or gorse bush or reed plant (for he is catholic in his nesting tastes) and he will but scurry off along the ground, cheating you into thinking that a mouse has run away. Yet in one afternoon on Sedgemoor I twice had the luck to locate from a distance a grasshopper warbler sitting on its eggs. One nest was in an unusually open site, and as I looked at the clump of herbage, up a short tunnel I could see the little brown-streaked bird incubating. And in the next marsh I saw another actually run on to its nest from a good ten yards away! But that was not the bird's fault. The osier cutters had been at work only a day before, and they had bared its nest to the sky with their clippers. Normally only the most diligent search will produce a nest, a search that will force you often on to your hands and knees before the lovely pink eggs are revealed in a nest that is deep buried out of sight.

Like so many skulking species, however, once the nest is found, it is possible to watch the grasshopper warbler with ease, for it is amongst the most confiding of birds. A little patience and a capacity to sit still will quickly admit you into his inmost secrets, and the elaboration of a hide is hardly necessary. One grasshopper I photographed regularly ran over my shoe on its way to its nest, nor was it for one moment disturbed while I was moving about setting up my camera. The chicks were fed as regularly as when I was hidden behind my canvas tent.

The big osier beds that are scattered over Sedgemoor are miniature jungles, rich in undergrowth of nettles, rush, meadowsweet and flags. They are the favourite haunt of the three British breeding *Acrocephali*—sedge, reed and marsh warblers. If there is any one species which in particular would take an ornithologist to Sedgemoor, it is the marsh warbler—unless perchance he searched its levels for a spotted crake, which has been proved to breed, and perhaps does so regularly.

The marsh warbler sets a pretty problem in bird identification. Chiff-chaff and willow wren, marsh and willow tits are but two other examples of similar problems. But not even these are as difficult to separate as the reed and marsh warblers, and it is little wonder that this species was overlooked for so long a time. Plumage distinctions are of little use. A dead bird held in the hand and closely scrutinized from all angles and in the best of lights will reveal the marsh warbler's lighter brown legs; and the olive green of its rump side by side with the rich brown of the reed warbler's might seem a character so distinct and definite that identification in the field might not appear difficult. Such is very far from being the case. In the first place it is only in flight that the rump of a bird is exposed for examination, and in a cover-loving species such views are at best only fleeting. In fact, in the thickness of the osier beds which are its summer home the marsh warbler flies but little. It progresses rather by hopping from perch to perch than by the use of its wings. Nor has it the helpful habit of sitting with its wings widespread as the cormorant does on an old post in the estuary. It is a quiet little bird that will peep at you round a withy and then slip off to another perch from which it will repeat the performance. Most of the time you will see little, except its head or its tail or part of its body. The rest is screened from direct view. Warblers are notoriously difficult to see to advantage, and if there is any species which requires the best of views for certain identification, it is the marsh warbler.

Apart from the intrinsic difficulties of seeing the bird at all the colours which are its hall-marks are those which are most subject to subtle alteration with the effects of light and environment. For one June and half a July I was in frequent company of this rare warbler, and for days I watched it at two nests from a range of but four or five feet. During this time I was much impressed by the manner in which the bird's tone was apparently affected by changes in light and environment. Bright sun, making the green of the herbage almost yellow, was reflected in a brightening of the green tones in the bird. At such moments it was obviously a marsh warbler—until a reed warbler passed by, and it too appeared to be lighter and greener. And vice versa; on days of shadows and of rain the bird became darker to the eye. Its greens became browns until I was left with the feeling that it was a minor chameleon. From that day I have felt that a field identification of this species which is founded on plumage distinctions alone must be suspect, however experienced and careful the ornithologist who expresses the opinion. Opinion at least I am certain it can only be, for he would be a rash bird-watcher who would stake his reputation on a foundation so uncertain as the olive green of the marsh warbler.

By what then are we to identify this mystery bird, and how can it ever be with certainty separated from its far commoner relative, the reed warbler? You can of course shoot it, but happily the day has gone, or at worst is rapidly going, when ornithologists refuse to believe their eyes until the specimen lies dead in the hand. 'It isn't a rough-legged buzzard till it's dead', said a famous nineteenth-century bird man to a friend who had the temerity to proclaim a large bird of prey to be of that species with the aid of his field glasses alone. We no longer think like that, and instead we turn to other methods less drastic but less harmful, and infinitely more pleasurable.

Various factors can be brought into use to assist in its identification. Song, nest, eggs, and habitat—all these help in varying degrees, and the art of the bird-watcher in proving beyond doubt to himself the identity of any species which calls for particular care lies in the correct use of all these and other threads of circumstantial evidence. Where doubts exist, they must be analysed by the consideration of all these and other aids.

The process is one of comparison and the intelligent balancing of circumstantial evidence. It has been said that these two species are the only British birds best separated by their nests and eggs, and there is undoubtedly much truth in this statement, for in this respect they differ widely. The paler ground colour and the larger blotches on the marsh warbler's eggs are quite distinctive from the less contrastedly marked greenish brown eggs of the reed warbler. The nests too are characteristic. That of the reed warbler is amongst the neatest and most elaborate of all British species. Its deep, tidy and finished nest, so compactly woven round the living reed stems, has been often described and frequently used as an illustration of bird architecture. In contrast, the marsh warbler builds an untidy and more loosely knit structure, much more like that which is typical of the true warblers, as for instance the whitethroat. Again, whereas the common bird so often uses reed fluff as building material, the rarer seldom builds with anything more than dried bents. The marsh warbler's nest has also one most distinctive feature. In the great majority of cases there are one or two pronounced 'basket handles' of building material, running from the edge of the nest and securely lashing it to some twig or leaf above it.

It is, however, few of us who find the nest of a species first and identify the owner afterwards, not at least in the case of rare birds. If we are so lucky, then our search for the marsh warbler is over, and it remains but to wait and watch, and the parents will soon be seen. But the cart is not often thus put before the horse, and normally it is necessary to locate the bird first and discover its secret afterwards.

As with so many birds, the song is the best method of approach. How often has every ornithologist found a bird, of which he would undoubtedly never otherwise have known the presence, by a sudden burst of song or a harsh alarm call from the dense undergrowth? It may be a call we at once recognize, of some species already familiar to us, or, as at times—and what great moments these are in a bird-watcher's history—it may be an unknown song which introduces us, when its author is tracked to earth, to a bird we have not seen before.

So it is with our present subject. Song is undoubtedly the first and best means of introduction to the marsh warbler, for although its calls and notes are in many ways reminiscent of the typical *Acrocephali*—and there are certain to be reed and sedge warblers near with which to compare it—yet in the marsh warbler many notes are introduced which lack the normal harshness, notes of a most pleasing quality and of fine musical appeal. It is also a great mimic. If phrases from a thrush's or a blackbird's song, or the call of a goldfinch suddenly issue from your bird, be not surprised. They will serve you in one more little way, to feel the more sure that the songster to which you listen is indeed the rare quarry you seek.

What of habitat? This is another factor which must always be considered in bird identification, and it can be circumstantially of the greatest assistance. Many textbooks will say that the reed warbler breeds normally over water, the marsh over dry land. Whilst I have never found the marsh warbler nesting over water, its relative is by no means so consistent, and in these Sedgemoor osier beds the normal site for reed warblers seems not to be in the growing reeds of the ditches but in the osiers themselves and amongst the nettles below: in short in almost exactly the same situations as its rarer cousin adopts. Indeed, the nests of these Sedgemoor reed warblers warrant a little more than a casual glance, for they are undoubtedly different from the normal neat cup so cunningly constructed amongst reeds. This type of site is of course found here along the reed-grown dykes. The great majority of the Sedgemoor birds, however, show a marked preference for the osier beds. Here they build in the withies themselves, as well as in the nettles of the undergrowth, often at no small height, at least for the species. Nests head-high are not infrequent, and on one occasion I had actually to *climb* off the ground before I could reach into the cup. Nests thus built are less tidy and symmetrical than those in reeds and, in order to be perverse, have at times traces of 'basket handles', enough to have made me more than once think they belonged to marsh warblers. In one season (1938), when the sheep had been grazing near by, a great number were constructed of wool, great fluffy grey balls swaying in the osiers. Nevertheless, on a critical inspection they are readily separated from the nests of marsh warblers, being bulkier, more carefully constructed and with more ambitious material. Even in a withy a reed warbler's nest is a masterpiece of bird architecture, a marsh warbler's rarely much more than a flimsy, rather precarious, structure.

One minor point is perhaps worthy of mention if only because the frequency of its occurrence forces me to conclude that it is a definite habitat preference of the species. Marsh warbler's nests are in my experience normally found in a narrow band round the edge of the withy beds. I have not seen one closer to the edge than four yards nor deeper in than eight. The reed warblers will often build in the middle, but not the rarer bird. On Sedgemoor at least it seems to have this limited habitat.

At the nest it differs little in habits from the reed and sedge warblers.

Both sexes tend the young. Male and female are alike and quite insepar-
able short of a post-mortem, but with chicks both certainly assist in
feeding. I have never seen the two birds change places on the eggs. Both
are equally scrupulous about nest-sanitation and after most feeds remove
excreta in their bills. Perhaps one other personal impression is worth
recording. In its carriage and many of its attitudes the marsh warbler
reminds me of a true *Sylvia* of the garden warbler type rather than an
Acrocephalus. Such impressions are often the whim of the individual who
states them, but where identification is so difficult, he is obstinate indeed
who is not thankful for even the most slender of straws that may help
him.

Such in brief survey is Sedgemoor's bird life. There are of course
other species than those which have been mentioned in these few pages.
Skylarks share the cattle pastures with the yellow wagtails and corn
buntings. Brown linnets and a few whitethroats are the unexpected
tenants with reed and sedge warblers of the osier beds. Corncrakes breed
regularly, even to-day, but as always they are wandering voices in the
deep undergrowth rather than flesh and feather before the eyes. Even the
rare spotted crake nests, and perhaps regularly. Mallard are common
nesters, and garganey have also been recorded breeding. But the characteristic large bird of Sedgemoor is the heron, whose attenuated grey
form is always to be seen fishing in the ditches or with slow beating
wings flying back to the wood on the high ground where he nests.

PLATE 91. *Buzzard with full-grown chicks*

PLATE 92. *Buzzard with chicks* 15 *days old*

PLATE 93. *Young Buzzards about* 40 *days old*

CHAPTER 8

An Exmoor Coomb

The birds of Exmoor are well represented in ornithological literature by the delightful prose of E. W. Hendy. His many chapters on them, written by one who lives in this lovely spot and knows it in all its moods, render more difficult, almost redundant, the task of the occasional visitor who feels inspired to add his share of praise. For of no locality can the birds ever be truly seen in correct perspective by him who is amongst them only for brief periods. The following is therefore no attempt at a comprehensive account of Exmoor, but rather a brief appreciation of many happy hours of peace in the company of its birds and in the restfulness of its deep coombs.

To one such as myself, for ever afflicted with a hill-hungry mind, the debt to Exmoor is great, and never greater than during the war, when the big hills were made more remote and inaccessible by the problem of travel and the shortness of leaves. For to the southerner with the hill-fever upon him Exmoor is indeed a blessing—a miniature region of mountains and moors, easily reached and in its valleys more lovely perhaps than even the real thing itself. I have never known Exmoor do aught but smile, even when wind and rain have tried their level best to spoil her charm. In her folds she holds these little coombs which by their perfect peace never fail to lift me into the higher planes of well-being and quietness of mind. There are places you can walk and never meet a soul all day, and if you are a true lover of the wilder places of this earth, you will be as selfish as I about the presence of your fellow-men, and as intolerant of any intrusion from the outside world. We go to the hills

93

for solitude. Exmoor can provide that solitude, yet never far from the good cheer to which it is always pleasant to return.

I first came to Exmoor to find the ring ouzel, a bird which has always attracted me. For reasons, the roots of which I never know, now this, now that bird has evoked within me the desire to seek, to find, to see. On that account my more serious-minded bird friends will never find in me a very stable contributor to ornithology, for the victim of such desires scratches only at the surface of each bird he chases. He lacks that consistency, that singleness of purpose which are indispensable to him who would aspire to a high place amongst the *élite* of modern bird study, whose work I read with greed and admiration, though to it I fear I shall at best contribute but tiny fragments. My bird star guides me to the chase and to the hunt—a distressingly reactionary attitude no doubt, yet one I could not jettison if I would.

Thus it was that in May I found my car parked for the first time on Exmoor on a high point in the middle of the moor, and that I first looked down the long winding valley which since then has often given me days of peace and quiet, and which I know by no name that the Ordnance Survey would recognize, but as Ring Ouzel Coomb. There is no valley on the rest of Exmoor which I like better; there could certainly be none more peaceful. Yet at first sight it has no essentially distinctive features, unless perhaps it runs through a deeper cleft than most. But the waters of its young stream seem to babble on their way more cheerily and cleaner than other burns, and its heather, bracken, scrub and scattered rowans seem to harbour a more numerous and varied population of birds than other valleys. Above all the ring ouzel lives there, and the mountain blackbird is a breaker of solitude that always delights me. Ring Ouzel Coomb for me is Exmoor. Slender indeed are my claims to chronicle the Moor's bird life, for it can rarely have had a more narrow-minded bird-pilgrim. Yet from E. W. Hendy's writings my valley would appear to be very representative of the birds of the truly moorland parts as opposed to the bigger and more luxuriant river valleys.

If you would descend my coomb, you will leave your car on the open moor and look over a half-mile of poor heather and moor grass to one of those lines of stunted beech trees which are everywhere on the Moor so much a feature of the landscape. And if your first bird is not a meadow pipit, there will be something amiss. For the open moorland of Exmoor knows this little pipit as its commonest inhabitant, as does every other moor I have travelled from the desolate peat hags of Shetland to Land's End. There are counties in which heath-land or rough commons with rank grass are not common, and in such the meadow pipit is almost a bird of note; Oxfordshire is one, except on the unkempt levels of Otmoor. But no moorland is complete without it. Often it has been my only avian companion for miles—a dull, dingy bird as it flushes in front of you and drops again into the heather, but our English fells and Scottish mountains would be the poorer for its absence. Here on Exmoor it abounds, and on March days, before even the stonechats have arrived, and when I have wandered down the coombs looking for ravens, it has been the meadow pipit's song alone that has cheered my way and made me realize that these places are not devoid of life.

Grouse too are here—Exmoor grouse, not a hardy breed, or at least so I conclude from their lack of increase. Yet it is a poor day upon which you do not flush one, and when you insult Exmoor, as I fear I have at times, by visiting her in the spirit that, as no real mountains are readily available, she will serve in lieu, it is good indeed to have so real a reminder of the true Highlands.

If you are lucky, you may get an even more efficient rebuff to your patronizing attitude with a blackcock. From my car one evening I heard the soft cooing of doves. For a moment I heard, and yet failed to remember. But only for a moment. These were no cushats in the beeches, but blackgame 'rookooing' at their lek. I was grateful for the low beech hedge which made easy my approach, and through it, as I lay full stretched, I watched no less than seventeen males, tails full-raised, busy at that odd display which is perhaps the most interesting bird spectacle to be seen in the British Isles. Seventeen cock birds! Three more even than at the tourney ground at which I studied them in Rothiemurchus under the shadow of the highest hills in Britain.

Thus can Exmoor surprise and revenge herself on those who visit her in patronizing mood. For the Moor is her own place. She neither expects nor suggests that she is mountain country, but asks only to be taken at her face value. Never since the incident of the blackcock have I so insulted her. I go there now chastened and as a pilgrim to Exmoor and not to a mere substitute for the northern hills.

And indeed Exmoor as a haunt of bird life can very well stand on her own merits, if only for the buzzards which she harbours. Is there any locality within these islands where you can see more buzzards or to better advantage than on these Somerset uplands? Wales? I think not. The country is vaster and the big birds more dispersed. On Exmoor they abound, if it is ever possible for a large bird of prey which requires big feeding territories to abound. Do not imagine that they circle like vultures over a carcass, for that is to expect too much. But in the wilder parts they are constantly to be seen soaring or hunting, and often, as the car passes, they will sweep out of a roadside beech which they have been using as a watch-tower. They are as common as the limitations of territory will permit them to be, and long may they so continue; for if you thirst for big birds and decry the lack of large birds of prey soaring in English skies, the buzzards of Exmoor will do much to slake you and to make you qualify your ideas.

I have always been at a loss to understand the distribution of the buzzard in Great Britain. There are miles of wilder country far than Exmoor where the buzzard is still almost uncommon. In the Border country, amongst the Grampians, in the many rocky valleys of north-west Sutherland I have never found it sufficiently numerous to warrant the description of common. The breeding pairs at least are widely scattered, and no man could pretend that it was abundant. Yet here in Somerset, and perhaps even more markedly in the wooded country of South Devon, often not far from the gay life of a summer holiday resort, the buzzard rules the skies. It is Exmoor's great bird glory.

At close quarters the buzzard is both a thrilling and yet a slightly disappointing bird. By virtue of its great size, if for nothing else, it is inspiring when seen for the first time from the close proximity of a hide, and I shall not readily forget the experience. Those who are inclined to regard bird photography as a pleasant, but perhaps not very useful, approach to the study of birds do not really know the great thrills which they miss by not sitting in hides. There is something about the view of a bird from a hide which makes all other forms of seeing birds unsatisfactory. It is not simply a matter of being so close; but rather the fact that through the restricted peep-hole in the canvas the watcher sees all bird and nothing but bird. It is his whole landscape, as it were, and there is little or no sky and few surroundings to distract the eye and merge the subject into the big world around it. That, the final climax of all the work attendant upon bird photography, and the fact that the camera can record such scenes, is the secret of its fascination. And with a bird like the buzzard the thrill of the first arrival is tremendous, as those great wings first close, and it stands there posed.

My excitement was all the greater because I had to wait long for the opportunity. Birds of prey, and especially the larger ones, feed their chicks at very long intervals, and in between their visits to the eyrie with food take no care for their young. Even torrential rain will not bring them back. It is not nervousness, but merely their Spartan code. I had spent two very long and fruitless sessions aloft on my buzzard before I glimpsed the parents. Clearly between 10 a.m. and 4 p.m. no meal was on the programme, and it was not until I got to the scene at daybreak that I was rewarded. The feeding interval of course varies with the type of food favoured. My pair fed largely on rabbits, and one rabbit was quite enough for two chicks for a lengthy period. Later in their development the cock bird was bringing reptiles (I saw both frog and slow worm), and consequently he came more often. But such prey demeans the buzzard. For that reason it is also a slightly disappointing bird. Like the vulture it is only lowly when it stoops to earth, to pick up reptiles, to feed on carrion, or at its best to snatch a cowering rabbit. Is it unfair to feel that the buzzard's majesty calls for a diet better suited to his noble appearance?

During the many hours of the adult's absence the growing chicks were a constant source of interest. From their earliest days, when they could have been no more than a week old, they practised that form of nest sanitation adopted by all the raptors. Although their legs could hardly support them, they would struggle to the edge of the eyrie, and propping themselves up on their stumpy little wings, evacuate with a long squirt over the side of the nest, until the branches surrounding it became very whitewashed.

The eyrie, too, was for ever brightened and garnished by twigs with fresh oak leaves. This is a well-known habit amongst eagles and buzzards, but I was interested to see the eyasses eating these fresh leaves. Can it be that such green stuff is brought to provide moisture and not to satisfy some mysterious instinct to adorn? Perhaps—but it must not be forgotten that many European raptors use coniferous twigs for this purpose, and whilst it is possible that a deciduous leaf might give moisture, it is difficult to think that pine needles could provide much. Yet the young certainly ate them, and no other explanation occurs to me.

Buzzards you will certainly see as you wander down the coomb of the ring ouzels, either perched on the beech hedge, soaring high above or planing over the heather at their hunting. You may also see the little merlin. On Exmoor, where the majority of the few breeding pairs, unlike their ground-nesting kinsmen of northern moors, use trees for nesting, the merlin is a rare bird. Near the ring ouzels there is every year a pair clearly breeding not very far away, though I have never found the old crow's nest which they must use. But the clean-cut, sickle-winged little tiercel often comes streaking down the coomb, low over the heather—a terror to the pipits and stonechats.

These small birds are indeed the real tenants of the ring ouzels' valley. The meadow pipits we have already mentioned. Let them be regarded for the rest of the walk as constant companions, for you will proceed only a few steps on your way without trespassing upon the territory of one pair after another. Wrens too are there, and that powerful song is possessed of increased volume in the close confines of the coomb. What a ubiquitous bird is the wren! As much at home in a town garden as in the woods, it adapts itself with equal ease to both moorland and the seacoast. You can see your wren hunting amongst rambler roses or playing the tree-creeper on a forest pine; you can see it singing from a precipice on the moor or amongst the rocks of the shore. Yet it is never out of place. There are few other birds to match it for catholic tastes in habitat. Here on Exmoor it is the noisiest inhabitant—unless perhaps a pair of curlews are busy at their courting.

Very different are the three chats—wheatear, whinchat and stonechat, of which there are evenly spaced pairs down the whole coomb's length, until a more luxuriant vegetation is reached. They make no pretence at regaling the moorland air with passionate song. They open their bills to curse, and flick their tails in alarm—the wheatear perched on a rock, the stonechat from a bracken frond, and the whinchat too, but his curses are mild beside the others': a more self-effacing bird, less assertive. He lacks that ample orange breast of the stonechat which gives such an impression of pompous dignity. His white eye-stripe gives him an air of surprise, and it would almost seem, when the two are nesting close together, that he intentionally retires behind the stonechat's more aggressive protection.

Where the valley bends and on the corner stands the lone rowan, in the old crow's nest of which I have always hoped the merlin would nest, a ring ouzel calls. How I love that call! It is so much a warning note, so very like the low cautionary whistle of one schoolboy to another when up to mischief and the danger of being caught threatens. How different too from the harsh scolding of the stonechat! You would think the ring ouzel meant to avoid detection, not force attention to the fact he has a nest for you to find, though, to be sure, when he has chicks fledged and in the heather, he forgets this earlier policy and will clatter round, shrieking with annoyance.

Yet his nest is not difficult to find. Here in this coomb there is a marked preference for building by a small rock jutting out of the peat, and above all where the heather, like a great lock of tousled, fallen hair, hangs over a rock, If you cannot find it there, you may have to show greater patience, for there are many steep banks to suit his tastes. But with chicks to be fed it is a simple matter, once you have thrown that vigilant cock bird off the trail, for he will follow you the length of the valley and see you off the premises in no niggardly fashion before he returns to his domestic duties. But with two people it is not hard to go one better than this intolerant gentleman with his white crescent set on black breast. Then he will return to play as big a part in the feeding of the chicks as his more soberly coloured mate. He is a gentleman of dignity, and only once, when he arrived with a moustache in the form of a young lizard, have I ever seen him in any other light.

CHAPTER 9

The Black Redstarts of Lowestoft

The spread and increase of the black redstart as a breeding species in this country is certainly the most spectacular and universally known event of British bird-life during the last decade. When a daily paper of popular tastes and policy can introduce a rare bird to its public with the title of 'the bird that follows the buzz-bombs', the notoriety which the black redstart has won for itself may rightly be judged to be significant.

Consequently its history has been fully written, and but a brief review of its story will suffice here. On the Continent it is a common bird of the towns and villages—especially in the Rhine Valley and in Switzerland, in the high mountain hamlets of which it is as the swallow is to us, the much-looked-for harbinger of spring and summer. In England it was first recorded by the late T. A. Coward as nesting in 1923 and 1924 'on the south coast' a deliberately vague locality, since disclosed as having been Sussex. In 1925 two pairs bred. Until 1929, when breeding first began in Cornwall, this remained the only known outpost of the bird, although it has since come to light that at least three pairs have bred regularly since 1927 in the old exhibition grounds at Wembley. In 1930, however, a pair bred in Kent, and in 1933 another pair at Woolwich. In the meantime, since 1927, the birds were present at South Kensington and elsewhere in Inner London, although at this date the existence of the Wembley 'colony' was not known.

It was not however till 1936 that the real spread seems to have begun, chiefly in London, hence the bird's fame. But in that year Cambridge was also honoured. By 1942 six breeding pairs of blac& redstarts were

PLATE 94. *Male Ring Ouzel with lizard*

PLATE 95. *Female Ring Ouzel*

PLATE 96. *Black Redstart at window*

known, and in 1943 this number had risen to ten, and the bird had even reached Warwickshire. At this date the City of London itself could claim three nests in, of all places, the Temple, the Charterhouse and Fetter Lane.

First reactions to this spread and increase which had been most marked during the war were to attribute their cause to the blitz. While the bombing of London undoubtedly assisted by making available an inexhaustible supply of breeding places and led to the creation on the bomb-damaged sites of many little natural weed gardens with their attendant insect life, it can at best have been only a contributory factor. It is abundantly clear that the species was earlier on the upward grade of a wave of expansion, and the recently disclosed evidence of its regularity since 1927 at Wembley would seem to indicate the reservoir from which the London birds of 1927 onwards originally came.

It is clear that the black redstart was increasing and spreading on its own account, and that the presence of blitzed buildings and the attendant suitable nesting sites can only have contributed to, not caused, the present position. There can be little doubt that we are winning this redstart as a new breeding species, and that with the end of the war, with observation in a thorough manner without let or hindrance and with above all the unrestricted use of field glasses, it will prove to be more firmly established than is at present known.[1]

I was stationed at Norwich when I was reading the report in *British Birds* on the black redstart in England in 1943. At that time I had seen very little of this bird. I remember my first. It was the end of term, and I was waiting for my people to pick me up from school for the holidays. A black redstart curbed my impatience as it flew about the stonework of Lancing College Chapel, descending at intervals on to the lawn in search of food. There was another I remember on a pollarded willow at the edge of Port Meadow when I was taking a Sunday afternoon 'constitutional' at Oxford. I had seen a little of the species on the Continent. But apart from those few glimpses it was as extinct as the dodo to me. In 1942 I had been invited by telegram to make a flying visit to photograph the bird in Inner London, but military duties had made that impossible.

[1] At the same time, it is clearly a capricious species and not yet very stable. Three pairs nested, all successfully, at Lowestoft in 1943. In 1944 there was only the one pair which reared two broods. Yet in 1945 Mr. F. C. Cook could find no black redstarts nesting in the town.

Bird Haunts in Southern England

The report of 1943 mentioned that no less than three pairs of black redstarts had nested successfully in that year in Lowestoft. I was at Norwich; Lowestoft but a short train journey away. Clearly I could not let such an excellent opportunity slip by, if in 1944 this little newcomer should once again favour that town with its presence. I wrote the recorder, Mr. F. C. Cook, to ask him if he could assist me. He most generously offered his help and, as will be revealed, later gave it in the most practical manner. At the same time a bird-photographer friend of mine, Captain B. Jeans, of the Royal Marines, found himself posted to a Combined Operations unit in Lowestoft. The fates were clearly with me. The vultures were gathering. . . .

Nineteen forty-four, however, had grimmer business to offer than the quiet peacefulness of watching rare birds. While the little redstarts were courting and beginning their nesting season, the whole of the effort of this country was being exerted towards D-Day and the greatest of all military operations. Work increased, and 'time-off' grew less and less. Yet there were hours of leisure. Unfortunately many other factors introduced complications. All leave was in abeyance; banned areas (including Lowestoft) were rigidly enforced; for military personnel there were distance limits for travel.

Still there *were* a few hours of leisure; there *were* black redstarts at Lowestoft, however banned it might be; I *had* two allies in the enemy's camp. . . . One May evening Jeans rang me up to say that Cook and he had located a singing cock black redstart. Could I come?

Could I come? I forgot banned areas, travel restrictions and the whole bag of tricks. A soldier who sat in an office and wrestled with administrative problems needed a little peaceful relaxation, and what better than bird-watching, even if it were at Lowestoft? As I told my C.O. if I were court-martialled 'in that he on 20th May 1944 did make illicit entry into Lowestoft and did see and photograph the black redstart', neither my regiment nor my family escutcheon would have to wear too disgraceful a bar sinister.

Of course I went. But how I cursed that evening course in wireless that made havoc of so many of our well-laid plans. When I did contrive to catch the evening train, I was dressed up to the nines in equipment, revolvers and the like, for an administrative type quite a soldier, in fact. Jeans, looking ditto, met me at the station. It was all very official, and there was in the background a Garrison Adjutant, whose interest in birds had also drawn him into the net, to give my visit the correct flavour of legality. We were past the scrutiny of the police in a moment and outside the station. I felt there ought to have been at least a staff car, but a rickety old Royal Marine bicycle served its purpose admirably.

The conspirators assembled for a council of war. The nest was not yet located, but the cock bird's singing perches had been noted. To my horror I first learnt that its chosen territory was not a district of unmilitary, suburban or everyday Lowestoft, but the very waterfront itself where preparations for D-Day were of course in progress. If Lowestoft itself was banned, how much more its waterfront? Still, as well be court-martialled for a sheep as a lamb. I began to think I would need my warlike equipment with which to shoot my way out.

We repaired to the 'breeding haunt'. This consisted of a number of burnt-out or very decrepit warehouses on the front. The male had been singing over an area which included about 200 yards of ruins or inhabited buildings, one of which very conveniently was a public-house.

Now the technique of black redstart nest-hunting is very different from that employed in the case of other rare birds I have pursued. If you can imagine the house sparrow as a great rarity and that you wished to find its nest, you will be able to visualize the difficulties and the embarrassments. Even with complete freedom of action you need a skin like a rhinoceros to knock at a front door, tell the owner he has a ramshackle sort of home ideal for a black redstart, and ask his permission to inspect his broken-down domain. A punch on the nose or internment in the local asylum would be the probable answer.

These, however, were not ordinary circumstances. We were there, where we had no business to be, as thieves in the night. We could not openly even use our field glasses, hidden in battle-dress blouses. Without them the ubiquitous house sparrows made an unmitigated nuisance of themselves. They seemed to delight in sitting on chimney tops or gables, silhouetted against the sky. Of course, they looked black: of course, they were the cock redstart—until they were sparrows. I cursed the whole race of *Passer domesticus*. They seemed to take a fiendish delight in posing as their distinguished neighbours.

Of course, too, the cock bird decided that it was no day to sit on a roof-top and sing. He would. Sparrows chirruped: even a blackbird in a garden sang a few notes: swallows flew by twittering: swifts screamed in the first joy of their return—but not a sound from *Phoenicurus ochrurus*.

One of the boundaries of his territory, however, was an old warehouse where Cook had found him breeding in 1943. I decided to search this in the hope of a stroke of luck. Now, if circumspection had been called for when one was in the street beneath in order to avoid attracting unhealthy attention, poking one's head out of the roofless top of somebody else's old warehouse and communicating the negative results of one's search to companions forty feet below is asking at any time for curiosity, if not indeed to be put behind bars. The method lacked finesse. I gave it up, and contented myself with inspecting last year's site and wishing conservatism was a characteristic of the black redstart.

We took to loitering in the street, hoping that the cock would sing and give us a clue. He remained silent. We continued to stroll up and down, talking about all sorts of military matters, a perfect little military reconnaissance party—or so we thought. Not so, however, a certain gentleman who was alternately propping his back against or stropping it on the door of the public house, waiting for the witching hour of opening time. As we passed him for the tenth time, he approached us, and without beating about the bush asked if we would like to see the redstart's nest.

I nearly fell through the earth. Then we all laughed. I began to be glad the military fates had not decreed for me a spy's job, for it was clear that by now I would long ago have faced a firing squad. It was really too ridiculous. Here was a perfectly normal civilian who had seen straight through us, our appearance and our conversation, and who was asking us if we would like to see not just the black redstart itself, but its nest!

From his confidence, however, I knew our search was at an end. And it was so. He led us into an empty but comparatively undamaged warehouse immediately opposite the pub, up two flights of old stairs and into an attic. There he calmly pointed to a nest on the lintel and departed, suitably rewarded both for his assistance and, we hoped, his future silence on our presence and activities.

By such means and in such places are modern British rare birds found nesting!

The nest contained three newly hatched chicks. It was surprisingly bulky, sited more like that of a swallow, but composed of moss and grasses. Outside was a courtyard, and on the roof of an adjoining outhouse a pair of black redstarts, to make assurance doubly sure, were growing exceedingly anxious.

The Black Redstarts of Lowestoft

Now it was one thing to get myself into Lowestoft and above all into its waterfront, see the black redstart and locate its nest. It was quite another to return myself to Lowestoft with the addition of a camera and a hide and the necessary photographic paraphernalia. Fortunately I had allies in the camp, and without the unstinting work which both Jeans and Cook put in in my absence on my behalf, my experience of the black redstart would have ended with the man who propped up the public-house door.

But first I had to decide whether I *ought* to photograph the bird. I was not struggling in the least with my public conscience, banned areas, cameras forbidden, grim business on hand. All that had long since gone overboard. Really rare birds, however, or those like this redstart which are just striving to expand themselves, are best left as undisturbed as possible. The photography of birds, however careful its application, *must* by the nature of its work introduce disturbance, and with disturbance there must always be also some risk. Where the risk is considerable, the camera should never be introduced. But there are birds and birds. Such species as kite and marsh harrier, two of our rarest breeding birds, are excessively nervous and resentful of intrusion. They should be left in peace. But the black redstart is in a very different category. It likes man's proximity so much that it deliberately selects his company for nesting. Any doubts I had on the ill-effects of disturbance were hastily removed when one of the birds alit on the window-sill and almost asked us to move to one side so that it could fly directly up to the nest and feed its chicks.

We did a rapid reconnaissance. The nest itself was in a very poor place for photography. In peace time, with proper gear and transport and with freedom of action and with time, a good job could have been done at it with flashlight, and with the aid of a table to get the hide up to the right level. But my camera and hide alone were going to be a sufficient headache. Under the conditions under which we had to work the introduction of a furniture van was out of the question. It might seem that application in the right quarter would have legalized our most innocent activities. But I knew military applications. The chicks would have flown and left the vicinity before even a refusal had come through. Besides, if our request was turned down, 'illicit' work would have been out of the question, certainly more dangerous.

At least there was the window-sill on which the bird clearly perched.

She had—or so we at first thought—three lanes of entry, by one of two windows or a door. One window and the door were easily denied to her by the simple process of shutting both.

We decided on that course of action and departed to consider the other administrative problems. These consisted of getting the very forbidden camera from Norwich into the warehouse; a hide, and introducing it to the bird; and finally getting myself backwards and forwards between Norwich and Lowestoft. The last problem was easy. Battledress and equipment clearly covered a multitude of sins at the railway station. And if equipment was worn, then instead of military impedimenta it could conceal my camera and tripod. Cook very sportingly offered to keep the camera at his house once it was 'in', until the end of operations.

The hide was the problem. I did not want to appear to be moving in with camp bed and all. Cook again removed that difficulty by volunteering to make a rough one. Jeans and he offered to get it introduced to the bird during my absence.

The following week-end, part of which I had intended to spend in Lowestoft, saw me away on duty at Command Headquarters—an unforeseen stroke of bad luck. By my absence, however, I missed no picnic. The hide was introduced and of it the birds, as had been anticipated, took not the least notice—except that, being mounted near the window-sill, they preferred to avoid it by pointing out to us that besides the window there were countless holes in the roof through which entrance to the attic could be obtained! They also made it quite clear that with the hide where it was they preferred this method of approach. For the whole of the Sunday afternoon Jeans worked like a black, and I gather looked like one, in blocking those innumerable holes with old tiles, paper and anything on which he could lay his hands. I missed that part of the party and I am very much indebted to him for his labour. But eventually the work was done, and the redstarts were forced to use the window, which they did without demur.

When I arrived on the scene, the hard labour was over, the hide up and the birds using the entrance by the window without any hesitation. At this point the purely photographic difficulties began to raise their ugly head. In the first case a window-sill is not only a wide affair, but it is also quite deep. The birds had no particularly favoured part on which they liked to perch. Sometimes they used one end of the sill: sometimes the other: occasionally the centre. Often they flew straight into the nest. Sometimes they alit on the outer side of the sill: sometimes on the attic side. It was impossible to know whereon exactly to focus. In addition there was the problem of light. However bright it is outside, the exposure of a negative from the inner darkness of a room towards outer brightness must lead to lack of frontal lighting and pronounced back lighting.

The first problem we overcame in part by providing a suitable perch, a thin lath of wood nailed to one side of the window and jutting out into space at an angle of about forty-five degrees. Both birds were most obliging in their ready acceptance of this improvisation. Unfortunately it did not protrude far enough from the walls of the house to remove the lack of frontal lighting, and the resulting photographs were a mere caricature of black redstarts, black on breast and side and *white* on the back.

It was obvious that the situation really called for the use of flashlight. Now although I contrived to see my way through military service with a maximum of photographic kit, such things as reflectors and synchronizers were not included in my outfit. They were stored out of reach at home. However we decided to construct a new type of perch and to try to borrow the bare necessities for flash work.

The new perch was a monstrosity of the first order. It consisted of a T-piece of aged wood, to look as much like a bit of old rafter as possible, nailed at right angles to a longer piece of wood which we nailed to the centre of the sill, the T-piece sticking well out into the open and hanging over space. Unless the birds perched at the tip of the cross pieces of the T, it was useless. I certainly was not going to show a photograph even of a black redstart, perched in the middle of such a horrible piece of artificiality! If I could borrow the necessary flash gear, it was our intention to use this also on this same perch, which, if better than the first, still did not wholly solve the problem of the lack of frontal lighting.

I arrived for the final day's work to hear that both birds were making ready use of the monstrous perch, although they not infrequently gave it a complete miss and flew straight indoors. I first of all began by working the bird by normal day-lighting. In their use of the strange perch both birds were singularly obliging when one considered the number of alternative perches which were open to them. Above all, they seemed to prefer to perch on the tips of the T-crosspiece.

I had, however, succeeded in borrowing a flashlight reflector and in buying a few bulbs—but unfortunately no synchronizer to fire the flash bulb and camera shutter at the same time. As even on the new perch the lack of frontal lighting was pronounced, I determined to finish Operation Black Redstart by an attempt to flash the subject.

The final few hours ought certainly to have earned at least the curiosity of the authorities. The hide was mounted right in the open window of the attic: a great reflector stared out into space: periodically a brilliant flash would burst forth. The whole looked down over an enclosed yard of the warehouse onto A.A. guns, barrage balloons, ships and other warlike objects. There were sentries on duty, other troops strolling about: some playing football. Yet for four hours we continued work, and there was never a sign of curiosity—not even from the birds.

The final stage was almost the worst part of the whole operation. As will be clear, during my various hurried visits a considerable amount of photographic kit had been accumulated by degrees in the warehouse. At the end I decided to get out in one move. Cameras, hide, tripods, changing bag, plates, flash gear, all were to go back in one to the other side of the banned area. How we got it all to the station I do not quite know. The bicycles groaned under the weight—but not as much as I myself did when on my own I got off the train at Norwich looking like a Christmas tree. Operation Black Redstart was over.

In all I could make but three visits to the nest, and those three visits were so much hampered by the problems and work I have described, and, except for the last day, so curtailed in time, that my opportunities for observation of the birds were very restricted. The black redstart is one of the few birds I have photographed in which the operations of photography did definitely militate against observation, and my notes of my one intimate acquaintance with this little bird are a disgrace, a first-class example of how *not* to carry out bird photography.

The black redstart, however, is not an inspiring bird. It has the appeal which rarity will always have, and its present expansion, above all its use of London and the great haunts of man, forces it into the public eye; but the bird itself does not inspire. Perhaps I was peculiarly unfortunate in my pair, for the cock bird, which abroad I have seen in full plumage, black with white wing spots, was very immature. Only by his song and after very close scrutiny could he be separated from his dingy-brown, fire-tailed female. Several observers sat in the hide and saw both birds at close quarters, and all were impressed by this similarity in plumage and

PLATE 97. *Black Redstart—The first perch*

PLATE 98. *Black Redstart—The view through the window, 2nd perch*

PLATE 99. *Female Black Redstart*

the difficulty of separation. Cock black redstarts, immature in plumage, yet breeding and fertile, are apparently not uncommon. The male of my pair only began to put on his full dress in the autumn moult after a second brood had been raised in the basement of the warehouse.

Both male and female fed the chicks at the rate of about six visits between them per hour, chiefly on caterpillars which they obtained from the waste ground surrounding the warehouse and occupied by the barrage balloon. By one mannerism I was impressed, their steadiness. The common redstart is a very restless bird, constantly flirting its fire-red tail. Not so its rarer relative. In fact I have seen no small passerine bird whose movements were slower. On arrival at the nest with food it would freeze for many seconds at a time and in feeding the chicks there was nothing hurried. Again, it waited patiently for excreta to be produced, picked it up deliberately, carefully balanced it in its bill and flew off outside. Only when they saw us in the attic near the nest did either of the birds become restless. Then they would sit on the roof of the out-house opposite and curse us with harsh alarm notes, popping in and out of the tile-holes and open windows, flirting their tails in anxiety.

Yet if the bird itself was a slight disappointment, never before have I had so much fun, so much hard work, so many administrative problems to settle in photographing a bird. As a friend remarked, if anybody wanted positive proof of the dangerous madness of bird photographers, he has only to read this account of Operation Black Redstart.

Index

Index